PHIL REDMOND'S
20 YEARS OF BROOKSIDE

PHIL REDMOND'S
20 YEARS OF BROOKSIDE

CARLTON BOOKS

Every effort has been made to acknowledge correctly and contact the source
and/or copyright holder of each picture, and Carlton Books Limited apologises
for any unintentional errors or omissions which will be corrected in future
editions of this book.

Printed and bound in Italy

10 9 8 7 6 5 4 3 2 1

CONTENTS

INTRODUCTION by Phil Redmond

In a television age that is becoming more and more competitive and increasingly heavily regulated I am extremely proud to be celebrating *Brookside's* twentieth birthday. The programme's continuing success and its great achievement in notching up twenty years can be attributed to many things – the quality of writing, the performances, the production – however, I think *Brookside's* greatest asset is its distinctiveness.

From its very first day, I wanted *Brookside* to be different. As a dramatist, I was interested in tackling contemporary issues, and doing so in a manner that was challenging, thoughtful and sometimes provocative but above all entertaining (and I make no apology for that). That desire still drives the programme in 2002.

Twenty years ago, I introduced *Brookside* into a society hugely different from today. The concerns that informed the series then were issues such as long-term unemployment, women's position in society, the black economy, unions and their role in the workplace and the micro-electronic

technological revolution (a phrase that sounds almost quaint in the twenty-first century) and its effect upon work and leisure. As the years have passed, *Brookside* has reflected changing concerns and trends, emerging from the eighties into the less didactic nineties and now on into the new century.

What has remained a constant, however, is *Brookside's* passion to continue presenting stories reflecting the lives of real people, their concerns and problems. Sometimes it touches a nerve, sometimes it may even be considered controversial, but throughout, *Brookside* has remained a programme that has never been afraid to speak out, never afraid to tackle the most difficult of issues (even if sometimes this has made it unfashionable!). Alongside this it will also occasionally do something explosive, because *Brookside* is there to entertain.

Another consistent feature throughout the last twenty years has been *Brookside's* distinctive mix of characters. From the start I knew I wanted a range of people from different socio-economic groups living next door to one another. Apart

from reflecting the changing culture of modern day Britain, I also realised this would allow *Brookside* to tell many different stories from varied viewpoints: stories of people on their way up and people on their way down; stories across the class, gender and age ranges, and often providing different perspectives on the same subject matter (ex-executive Paul Collins and school-leaver Damon Grant both suffering through unemployment, for example). By establishing this microcosm from the very first episode I believe that over the years *Brookside* has been uniquely placed to reflect a wider range of experiences than any other continuing serial on television. It still serves the programme well today.

Brookside's twentieth birthday is, of course, an excellent excuse to look back over how far the programme has come – and there is nothing wrong with a little nostalgia. This book, however, is not just a retrospective; it is also an opportunity for *Brookside* to state its case. As we follow the series' fortunes year-by-year from 1982 up to the present day, we can also see

how it has managed to reinvent itself to remain relevant. So successful has this process been that *Brookside* in 2002 is as exciting and dynamic as it was when it premiered on the first night of Channel Four twenty years ago.

As I said, there is nothing wrong with a little nostalgia, and whilst we take an affectionate look at the past I am also looking to the future. 2002 brings me almost full circle with *Brookside*. I am back at the helm again, looking for new ways in which the series can innovate and push forward, new subjects it needs to address and new ways of telling our story. I am as proud of the stories that feature in *Brookside* in 2002 – from Anthony Murray's bullying storyline, to Jimmy Corkhill's mental health problems, to Dr Gary Parr's frustration with the NHS, to the dramatic events occurring during the programme's anniversary week – as I am of any throughout the series' history.

Stay tuned – there are a few surprises up ahead.

Paul Collins, moving in

BROOKSIDE: Episodes 1-18
WRITERS: Phil Redmond, Andy Lynch,
Jimmy McGovern, Allan Swift

DIRECTORS:
Chris Clough, Chris Lovett, Keith Washington

TRANSMISSION: November 2 – December 29

1982

HOUSE BY HOUSE

5 Union leader Bobby Grant is unhappy with management at his work, Fairbanks Engineering, and strike action begins over Christmas to prevent the loss of 200 jobs. Karen's boyfriend 'Demon' Duane tries to force her to have sex. Barry seeks revenge, but later, when Duane stabs him, he refuses to identify his attacker to police. The Grants stage a party at the end of the year, with the residents seeing in 1983 as they conga around the Close.

Karen Grant

8 The down-on-their-luck Collins family arrive at Brookside Close, downsizing from their plush lifestyle to find their house vandalised and their toilet stolen. Immediately they accuse Damon Grant, and in so doing, ensure their relationship with the Grants gets off on the wrong foot. Shortly after moving in, Paul returns from signing on to discover that they (along with the whole Close) have been burgled. Lucy is unhappy and bullied at her new school, but gains the upperhand wielding a hockey-stick. Upset at her family's reduced circumstances, she spends Christmas with friends on the Wirral. At the Grants' New Year's Eve party Annabelle talks Roger Huntington into helping her set up a Ratepayers Association.

Barry is stabbed

New Year on the Close

Lucy and Gordon Collins

The Collins – Annabelle, Paul, Gordon and Lucy

Paul Collins

Lucy lashes out

Heather Huntington

9 Highly-strung Roger Huntington is disturbed when, at a Law Society dinner, he sees a senior partner make a pass at his attractive wife, Heather. Prompted by the burglary, Roger installs an alarm, but the house is broken into again, and all the Christmas presents stolen.

10 Wheeler-dealer Gavin and Petra Taylor are trying for a baby. Gavin is selling second-hand cookers from his garden, which annoys snooty Paul Collins and Roger Huntington.

Gavin Taylor's cookers

COUNTDOWN TO BROOKSIDE

It's just after 4pm on November 2, 1982. Channel Four has taken to the airwaves for the first time. As continuity announcer Paul Coia introduces its first ever programme – *Countdown* – expectations are high. According to pre-publicity, Channel Four will bring us a new kind of viewing experience with challenging programmes designed to appeal to audiences normally ignored by British television. Central to this bold new plan will be the twice-weekly drama serial, *Brookside*. It will debut later that night at 8pm. But the *Brookside* story doesn't start there...

FROM QUANTITY SURVEYING TO GRANGE HILL

In 1973, Phil Redmond quit his job as a quantity surveyor to pursue a career in TV script writing. After first joining the writing team of *Doctor in Charge* (along with such comic talents as John Cleese and Graeme Garden), he developed an outline for a new drama serial that followed the lives of a group of residents on a new housing estate. The idea was submitted to various ITV companies, but none of them saw its potential. Pitching it to the BBC, he received the same response, and so the proposal remained in his 'ideas drawer' for the next eight years.

In the meantime, Redmond busied himself producing scripts for the children's serial *The Kids From 47A* and the office sitcom *The Squirrels* (working alongside Kenneth Cope, who would join the cast of *Brookside* in 1999 as Ray Hilton).

In 1976, having just completed a degree in social studies at the University of Liverpool, Redmond came up with a new idea: a children's drama serial that would present a realistic look at life in a secondary school, rather than the 'Boy's Own' approach that had been the normal way of portraying school dramas up until that point. He took his idea to Anna Home, an Executive Producer at the BBC, who immediately commissioned it. *Grange Hill* was born. The programme would grow from its nine-episode 'pilot' in 1978 to become one of Britain's longest-running children's drama serials (and in 2002 return 'home' to Phil Redmond when Mersey Television took over production of the series).

At times controversial, *Grange Hill* proved a great success. It also displayed many of the elements that would come to be recognised as typical of Phil Redmond's brand of television drama, with its tendency to tackle serious moral and social issues in a thoughtful, unsentimental manner; and brilliant story-telling.

THE FORMATION OF CHANNEL FOUR

In the early eighties, plans were underway for the creation of a fourth terrestrial television station in the UK, to be called Channel Four. Jeremy Isaacs, former Controller of Thames Television and Producer of the acclaimed documentary series, *The World at War*, was awarded the role of Chief Executive of the new channel and it was to be his job to seek out and commission programmes for the new network.

Channel Four was intended to be unlike any other TV channel before it – it would make no programmes of its own, instead acting as a kind of publishing house, commissioning work from independent producers. In 1981, Isaacs gave a speech to the Royal Institution of Great Britain, designed to brief independent producers about the

Tucker Jenkins in Grange Hill (© BBC)

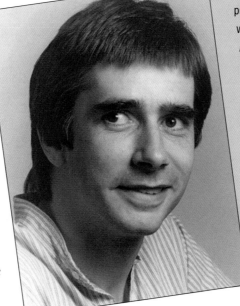

PHIL REDMOND

Born in 1949 on a council estate in Liverpool, Phil Redmond was among the first two percent of the population to attend a comprehensive school. In 1968, he left to work as a trainee quantity surveyor but four years later, decided to concentrate on a career as a scriptwriter. After contributing comedy scripts to, amongst others, Les Dawson, Harry Secombe and the *Doctor in Charge* television series, he returned to education as a mature student at the University of Liverpool. He took a degree in social studies – a move which reflected the keen social conscience that has informed his work ever since.

In 1978, Redmond created the innovative BBC children's series, *Grange Hill* (which later spawned the successful spin-off, *Tucker's Luck,* in 1983) and in 1981, devised *Going Out* for Southern Television. The same year he established his production company Mersey Television, through which he launched the pioneering drama serial, *Brookside,* for Channel Four in 1982.

Since then, Mersey Television has produced a second ongoing drama for the network, *Hollyoaks*, and many *Brookside* videos and spin-offs, as well as *Waterfront Beat* for the BBC, and *And The Beat Goes On* for Channel Four. In some senses, Redmond's career turned full circle in 2002, with Mersey Television taking over the production of *Grange Hill* for the BBC.

Today the company remains Britain's biggest permanent employer in the independent production sector.

new venture. When it was over he was approached by Redmond who challenged him on whether he would allow bad-language in a television drama if it were used in a realistic context. Isaacs confirmed that if it was dramatically justified he would. Satisfied, Redmond promised he would be handing him a format for a new drama in the next few weeks.

THE CREATION OF MERSEY TELEVISION

Whilst working on Grange Hill, Phil Redmond had often found himself at loggerheads with the BBC. There were arguments over the script, which he felt threatened the integrity of the programme; and he grew increasingly frustrated at having to let someone else have the final say on how the programme should be produced.

During this time he was also developing another programme for the corporation, *County Hall*, a weekly drama serial about local government. When the programme was commissioned, Redmond was concerned that the BBC team did not understand county council politics and were confusing it with the 'Town Hall'. In addition, the series' length was cut from the proposed 26 episodes to 13.

Redmond had also been developing the school-leavers drama, *Going Out*, for the ITV company, Southern Television. By comparison, this process had gone superbly well, the programme being properly budgeted and given a Producer/Director whom Redmond admired. Comparing the two experiences brought home to him just how much his work was subject to the whim of other people. He decided that the only way to maintain complete control over his own programmes was to establish his own production company.

The creation of Channel Four finally gave Redmond the opportunity to take what he described as 'the Marxist ethic of seizing the means of production' and to set up his own independent production company. He went to the Department of Trade and Industry for a grant, but found that he didn't qualify because he wasn't a manufacturer. They did, however, give him an assistance grant on the grounds that he was setting up in Liverpool and creating 70 jobs. It was enough. Jeremy Isaacs from Channel Four agreed to back the project and Mersey Television was founded.

Left: Wardrobe and technical block
Left below: No.10 and No.9
Below: Mersey TV's canteen

Brookside Close

BROOKSIDE CLOSE

Phil Redmond has credited his background in quantity surveying for the decision to purchase 13 houses as his permanent 'set' for Brookside. Some quick calculations had shown such a move would be cheaper than maintaining the continual costs of set construction and storage.

He arranged to meet with builders who were working on Lord Sefton's old estate in Croxteth, Liverpool. A cul-de-sac with the River Alt running alongside it caught his eye as the ideal location – and settled the programme's name for good: *Brookside.* Initially the name given to the drama had been *Meadowcroft* which Redmond felt echoed the pastoral-sounding names often given to housing estates. Unfortunately, Channel Four had already commissioned another programme called *Meadowlark*, and so Redmond agreed to alter his title. 'Meadowcroft' later lent itself to the name of the Close's residents' favourite soap: 'Meadowcroft Park'.

Gallery

MERCHANDISE

The first piece of bona-fide *Brookside* merchandise ever issued reached the shops in November 1982. A mere fortnight after the transmission of *Brookside's* first episode, the novel, *Brookside: Moving In,* by former Fleet Street Features Editor Colin Northway was published by Severn House Publishing. Telling the story of the first days on the Close, the publishers had approached Phil Redmond with the idea of producing a book after enjoying success with a series of novels based on his previous creation, *Grange Hill.*

Alongside the economic advantages, shooting in real houses gave the programme an extra degree of reality. Redmond ensured the houses on Brookside Close were designed to allow easy access for recording and camera equipment.

Of the 13 properties bought, seven were used for housing various aspects of the soap's production: three were offices, three housed technical facilities, and one contained a canteen. Redmond recalls that the average cost for set construction was going to be around £13,000 per episode. As each of the houses only cost £25,000 he reasoned that they would 'pay for themselves' in a matter of months.

THE FIRST CAST

Shooting began for episode one of *Brookside* on September 6, 1982. Gathered together were a group of actors, some of whom had little in the way of previous professional experience. The programme's first cast were selected by Phil Redmond and Janet Goddard. A full-time Casting Director – Dorothy Andrew – would not be appointed until a year after production started (Andrew has remained with the company to the present day).

Of that cast, Sue Johnston (Sheila Grant) had a cameo appearance in *Coronation Street* to her name, plus experience of work in community theatre. Two of the McGann brothers were initially cast as Barry and Damon Grant, but contractual problems meant the roles were ultimately given to Paul Usher and Simon O'Brien – for O'Brien this was to be his debut in professional acting. Jim Wiggins (Paul Collins), meanwhile, could boast of a couple of appearances in *The Professionals* and *Tales of the Unexpected*, and Rob Spendlove (Roger Huntington) also claimed a role in *Tales...* However, like Simon O'Brien, for the majority of the cast, *Brookside* was to be their first taste of a professional acting career.

This ensemble of relative unknowns would give the programme an added element of freshness when it reached the screens. No one brought any prior baggage to the role, or encouraged preconceptions in the minds of viewers. Come November 2, *Brookside* would speak for itself.

'WE'RE GONNA BE FAMOUS!'

A school friend of Paul Usher recalls sharing a drink with him and some of the cast shortly before the first episode went out. Paul

Gordon Collins

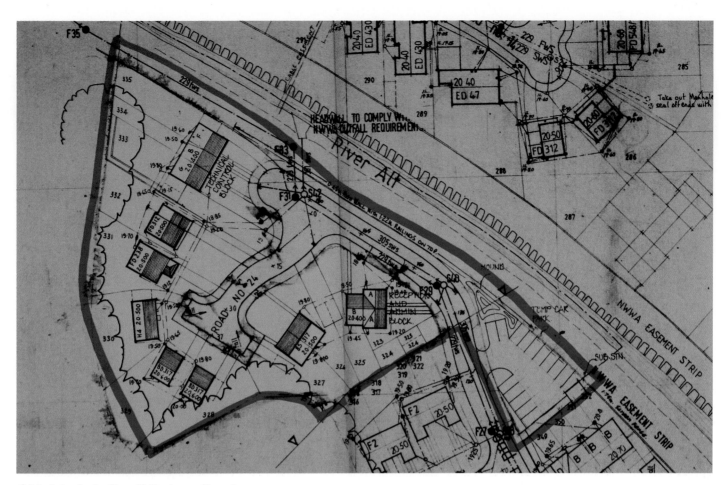

Original plan for the Close (© Persimmon Homes)

was in high spirits: 'In a few weeks time we're gonna be famous!' he claimed. His friend was not so sure. 'Famous? On a weird new channel that no one's going to watch? You bunch of unknowns? Yeah, right!'

Over at Channel Four, Jeremy Isaacs also had some reservations about the programme. Although considering it a 'quite remarkable achievement, created from minimal resources' he was concerned about the poor-quality of the sound. In actual fact this was because of a vital piece of equipment being delivered late to Mersey Television. Redmond remembers the irony: 'We had gone for an innovative cutting edge system, relying mainly on Japanese manufacturers. They delivered on time. The British guys didn't. It was also my harsh baptism in the perils of technological interference problems'. Having invested so much money in *Brookside* (plus awarding Mersey Television a three-year contract) Isaacs was willing to give Redmond and his team some time to sort out these early teething troubles.

Initial viewing figures were good, with ratings recorded of 4.2 million in November 1982, but this soon fell away when the traditional soap audience discovered that this was a programme with an attitude. *Brookside* was too harsh, too real and at times too uncomfortable for some viewers.

Perhaps inevitably, though, the press were quick to predict the programme's apparently imminent cancellation. On Boxing Day, *The Star* confidently reported: 'The Channel Four soap opera *Brookside*, plunged into controversy by the use of four-letter words, will be scrapped.'

REACTION

Initial reaction to *Brookside* was – in part – a mixture of shock and confusion. Switching on at 8pm on Channel Four's opening night, viewers perhaps expected a more sedate, homely programme than the raw television they were confronted with.

From the outset, Phil Redmond had almost promised the channel's Chief Executive Jeremy Isaacs bad language, and as far as some viewers were concerned, *Brookside* had it in abundance. And whilst this was part of Redmond's desire to pursue realism in the programme, it would become a bone of contention that would bother *Brookside* for its first nine months or so.

Alan Partridge

BROOKSIDE: Episodes 19–122
WRITERS: Phil Redmond, Chris Bernard, Frank Clarke, John Godber,
Janet Goddard, Andy Lynch, Jimmy McGovern, Len Rush,
Allan Swift, Helen J Wilson, Barry Woodward

DIRECTORS: Peter Boisseau, Chris Clough, Keith Evans,
Pedr James, Chris Lovett, Nick Prosser, Bren Simson,
Richard Standeven, Keith Washington

TRANSMISSION: January 4–December 28

1983

Harry and Edna Cross

HOUSE BY HOUSE

5 The strike at Fairbanks Engineering ends, but despite a long campaign, the factory is shut down in November. Sheila is made redundant in March, and joins Annabelle's Ratepayers Association. Barry pursues Petra Taylor after Gavin's death, then, after getting sacked from his job at the building site for stealing materials, goes into business with Terry Sullivan. Irritated by Petra's continuing depression, Barry steals some charity money from Sheila and heads to London, returning later in the year.

6 Alan Partridge arrives in the Close in April. He asks his partner Sam (Samantha!) to marry him. She says no, but agrees to move in with him.

Sheila and Barry

The Jacksons move in

17

Harry and Edna

Brookside Close

Gavin dies

7 Harry and Edna Cross move into No.7 in November – and soon after, Damon and Gizzmo start 'mysteriously' moving their garden gnomes.

8 The Collins' economy drive continues, as Paul is unable to find a job. Annabelle becomes a supply teacher to boost finances, and in May, Paul has to trade his Rover for a Maestro. After a year out of work he becomes a Youth Opportunities organiser. Lucy gets more involved with CND, but tension between her and Annabelle prompts her to leave for France in August, returning for Christmas.

9 Roger's boss continues to make advances towards Heather, implying that her 'co-operation' could influence Roger's career. In June, however, his boss lets him know he will not be made a partner as soon as he hoped. Roger's affair with his client, Diane McAllister, is eventually exposed and he ends up losing both women. Heather passes her accountancy exams.

10 Gavin dies from a brain haemorrhage and Petra goes to stay with her sister, Marie Jackson. Petra is pregnant but later miscarries. By August, her depression deepens, and she disappears from the Close. Her sister Marie and family temporarily move into Petra's house and try to trace her. At Christmas they receive a card from her with a smudged postmark.

Terry Sullivan

The Close

TEETHING TROUBLES

Brookside was up and running, but there were teething troubles that needed to be addressed sooner rather than later.

Sound problems – due to the delay in acquiring the necessary audio equipment – were continuing to draw criticism. The 'hollow' acoustics of the sets persisted, even when the houses had been occupied for a few weeks and filled with furnishings. To remedy this, sound absorbent tiles were fixed to the ceilings and movable sound panels installed. But there were other headaches, not least a flock of hens that would stray regularly onto the Close and constantly interrupt recording. In a similarly ornithological vein, nearby residents on the estate complained that lights from the crew's night-shoots were waking the local birds too early, and that birdsong was keeping their children awake.

Phil Redmond was always keen to maintain a good relationship with *Brookside's* real-life neighbours on the housing estate. Before production began, he invited local residents to inspect the sets and offices, and gave them a tour of the Close. As a result, residents meetings became a regular part of life on *Brookside* ensuring that the programme's neighbours were kept informed of any plans that might impact upon the estate as a whole.

By May, the programme was feeling adventurous enough to stage its first 'overseas' shoot: a week-long stint in the Isle of Man.

Alan Partridge

Karen Grant

Harry and Edna Cross

PHIL REDMOND'S LAST EPISODE

1983 would feature the last episodes to date bearing the writer's credit 'Phil Redmond'. Redmond had penned the first 10 Brookside episodes himself before bringing on board a team of writers. The final batch of episodes credited to him concerned the breakdown in Heather and Roger Huntington's marriage, with the last of these broadcast on September 21. He wrote these four episodes in just four days. Over 90 episodes of *Brookside* had been completed by this stage, enough for Redmond to feel happy that everyone on board understood what he was trying to achieve with the series.

WRITING BROOKSIDE

Perhaps because Redmond was a writer himself, *Brookside* would remain a writer-led programme. The soap is rightly lauded for discovering new acting talent, but *Brookside* has also been responsible for giving some of Britain's most influential writers their first television commission.

John Godber, for example, would go on from *Brookside* to write *The Ritz* and *The Continental* for BBC2, and ultimately, through works such as *Bouncers*, *The Outsiders* and *Up 'n' Under*, become the second-most performed living playwright in the English language. Frank Cottrell Boyce, meanwhile, would move on to further success, creating the soap,

Springhill, for Sky One, *A Woman's Guide to Adultery* for Carlton and latterly writing the feature-films *Hilary and Jackie* and *24 Hour Party People*. In 1989, Kay Mellor also cut her teeth on the programme, and has enjoyed further success in the nineties and beyond with *Band of Gold*, *Playing the Field*, *Fat Friends* and *A Good Thief*. Val Windsor, meanwhile, moved from *Brookside* to novel writing, enjoying great success with *Telling Stories* (which she started writing while still working for *Brookside*) and *Saints and Warriors*. And Jimmy McGovern went on to create the crime serial *Cracker* for Granada, the school drama *Hearts and Minds* for Channel Four and the docu-dramas, *Hillsborough*, for Granada, and *Dockers*, for Channel Four, amongst others.

WEATHERING THE STORM

By the year's end, Brookside had weathered the storm of outrage and had also introduced to critical acclaim some hard-hitting storylines, such as Gavin Taylor's death, Petra's subsequent miscarriage and disappearance, Paul Collins' continued efforts to try and find employment, and the breakdown of Roger and Heather Huntington's marriage.

Brookside was here to stay.

REACTION

Unimpressed by Brookside's technically rocky start, John Whitney, Director-General of the Independent Broadcasting Authority (IBA), called Channel Four's Chief Executive Jeremy Isaacs to account. Whitney insisted that the programme was not good enough, and, crucially, that he could not envisage it ever attaining the standards he demanded. Aware that these were teething problems, Isaacs explained that the channel was committed to the programme and that, 'There are things you might not like about it, but they will get sorted out. This is already a series with a very strong appeal.' Already Isaacs appreciated that in *Brookside*, Channel Four had a valuable asset: a programme that would generate a strong following and bring in regular viewers.

Alongside this, Redmond decided to drop the bad language from the programme, reasoning that, as Isaacs put it, 'the essential character of Brookside lay in its understanding of human nature and experience rather than in swearing, and that no matter how naturalistic swearing is, it could be sacrificed.'

Marie and George Jackson

BROOKSIDE: Episodes 123–227
WRITERS: Frank Clarke, Chris Curry, John Godber, Andy Lynch,
Jimmy McGovern, John Oakden, Jimmy Oakes, Susan Pleat,
Kathleen Potter, Allan Swift, Helen J Wilson, Barry Woodward

DIRECTORS: Peter Boisseau, Sue Butterworth, Bob Carlton, Chris Clough,
Terrence Daw, Charles Harris, Phill Hill, Des McCarthy, Eszter Nordin,
Nick Prosser, Matthew Robinson, Richard Standeven

TRANSMISSION: January 3 – December 31

1984

HOUSE BY HOUSE

5 In January, Sheila sets up a non-registered employment agency. Matty Nolan helps her out with a job, but ends up being prosecuted by the DHSS for fraud. In May, Sheila finds out she is pregnant, and tells Bobby while they are on holiday in Spain. Bobby gets a job in the same chemical firm as Paul Collins, but his union position leads to conflict between the two. Damon has problems finding a job when he leaves school. Barry and Terry enter into dealings with local villain Tommy McArdle, and later provide a fake alibi for the perpetrators of a robbery at a local warehouse. It is George Jackson, however, who ends up framed for the crime, and despite Barry and Terry confessing to the police at the last moment, he is convicted. Tommy McArdle isn't pleased, and they end up in hospital. Barry decides to leave Liverpool for a fresh start.

George is sentenced

Terry and Barry

6 Sam asks Alan to marry her, then jilts him at the altar to go to Los Angeles. His ex-girlfriend Liz moves in temporarily, but when Alan discovers it's her fault he's been accused of plagiarism – after helping sell Gordon Collins' computer programs – he throws her out. Later Liz returns with a sinister friend who viciously attacks Alan. In July, however, Alan meets up with Sam again, gets married, and leaves the Close. Harry and Edna Cross then move in, followed shortly by Ralph Hardwick after he is widowed. Edna is threatened with legal action due to gambling debts.

7 Harry is upset to find out that his son Kevin is living with a divorcee and her child. In May, he has a severe angina attack, and has to move downstairs. In September, they move into the bungalow, and let No.7 to two nurses, Kate Moses and Sandra Maghie, and hospital porter, Pat Hancock.

George in the dock

Harry has a scare

8 Paul is threatened by one of his Youth Opportunities charges. In May, he gets a job with a local chemical firm. Annabelle, meanwhile, is diagnosed with hyperthyroidism in February.

9 Heather reverts to her maiden name, Haversham, when she starts a new job in May.

10 Marie has a visit from the police to say that Petra has committed suicide in Llandudno. She blames Barry. The Jacksons decide to stay at No.10. Their father turns up and tries, unsuccessfully, to take possession of Petra's house, but this is resolved by the discovery of Petra's will, which leaves the house to Marie. George Jackson unwittingly gives Tommy McArdle information he then uses to rob a warehouse; George is convicted for the crime and gets 18 months in prison. Marie starts the 'Free George Jackson' campaign.

Barry, battered

THE PRESS

1984 saw *Brookside* launch some of its highest-profile storylines yet, while at the same time the tabloids were discovering that their circulations could be boosted through reporting the plotlines of popular drama serials. These plots increasingly made high-profile stories for the press and in *Brookside's* case, levels of media hype previously unseen accompanied the writing out of two major characters. Petra Taylor's disappearance resulted in reports of apparent sightings of her across the country. When it came to dispatching George Jackson, however, *Brookside* really pushed the boat out.

'FREE GEORGE JACKSON'

The 'Free George Jackson' campaign got off to a hilarious start when it was scripted that George Jackson's supporters would hang a banner demanding his release from the top of St John's Beacon, a 125-metre (400ft) tower and one of Liverpool's distinctive landmarks, which, incidentally, can be seen in *Brookside's* title sequence. The design team had to climb the steps of the Beacon (the lifts were out of order) to get to the top, where they discovered that high winds had put paid to the plan. Luckily, they were able to improvise, scrawling the message on large sheets of paper and pasting them on the windows of the former restaurant. (The top of the Beacon is today occupied by Liverpool's radio station, *Radio City*.)

Marie Jackson

George Jackson on trial

George, awaiting sentence

As the 'campaign' picked up pace across the country the *Brookside* press office even took delivery of a fruitcake with a file in it. George Jackson T-shirts and graffiti appeared on bus shelters proclaiming his innocence – and there was even a 7" record release.

The single 'Free George Jackson' was credited to *Blazing Saddles*. Mersey Television's Head of Music, Steve Wright, recalls that the group consisted of Kevin McGarry (vocals) and Dave Rowlands (pedal steel guitar) from local country and western group The Hillsiders, and Malcolm Holmes from

Orchestral Manoeuvres in the Dark on drums. A promotional video to accompany the single was also shot, featuring the musicians on a Liverpool ferry.

The idea for a spin-off single was inspired by the inclusion of two buskers in the storyline (who were the sons of Marie's friend, Betty), seen trying to raise money for the 'Free George Jackson' campaign. Wright credits Phil Redmond with the notion of making a record, but no one can recall who came up with the moniker *Blazing Saddles*.

The 'Free George Jackson' campaign was a watershed for *Brookside*, representing the moment when the soap moved from cult status to a programme that would form a part of the national psyche. It is interesting to note that other drama serials would run similar-style campaigns, with even *Brookside* itself returning to the idea in 1995 with the 'Free the Jordache Two' storyline. Ultimately, George Jackson served his sentence and actor Cliff Howells left.

The campaign poster

MERCHANDISE

To tie in with the 'Free George Jackson' campaign, *Brookside* issued 'a potential chart-busting' record (as *The Sunday People* described it on December 9), a pop video protesting his innocence, a poster campaign accompanied by badges and T-shirts and a special telephone hotline which viewers could call to hear updates (recorded by Anna Keaveney who played Marie Jackson) of how George and the family were getting on. Alongside the George Jackson memorabilia, the *Brookside* theme tune was also issued on 7", with the B-side featuring two tracks – 'Theme from Everyman' and 'Mersey Mist'. This record was not generally available, however, being pressed purely as a momento of a charity show the *Brookside* cast performed at Liverpool's Everyman Theatre (hence the title of the first track on the B-side).

'FREE GEORGE JACKSON': THE LYRICS

He called in to his local,
Still shaken and in need
Of a quiet drink. A quiet think.
Disturbed by what he'd seen.
He didn't realise that the blaze
He'd fought that day
Was of interest to McArdle,
In some strange kinda way.

So free George Jackson
Free George Jackson
Free George Jackson
He's an innocent man

What's the sense in saying
We'd never have done the same
Because no one could have realised
What was McArdle's game.
That diagram on the napkin,
Has brought so much heartache
For this man and his family
That's why we're here to say.

So Free George Jackson
Free George Jackson
Free George Jackson
He's an innocent man

Set up by McArdle
Sent down by the Law
Barry and Terry have left him
And Marie to settle the score.

So free George Jackson
Free George Jackson
Free George Jackson
He's an innocent man

Pat Hancock, Sandra Maghie and Kate Moses

The Jackson twins with Davy Jones

Gary and little George Jackson

REACTION

There was a sense throughout 1984 that *Brookside* was approaching critical mass. Criticisms of poor production quality and bad language could no longer apply, and whilst the programme would still continue to be controversial thanks to its political and socially aware plots, the general response to *Brookside* was extremely positive.

As a mark of the show's appeal to a young audience, pop magazines *Smash Hits* and *No.1* voted *Brookside* the best programme of the year, while readers of the *NME* voted it their third favourite. In an article for *Marxism Today*, theorist Christine Geraghty criticised the series because: '[the] public world of work and unions is represented as being exclusively male and the women are presented as supporting their men rather than challenging them.' However *The Sunday People* was now hailing *Brookside* as 'the Rolls Royce of Soaps'.

Karen Grant

BROOKSIDE: Episodes 228–332
WRITERS: Janet Goddard, Andy Lynch, Alan McDonald,
Jimmy McGovern, John Oakden, Jimmy Oakes, Jan Needle,
Susan Pleat, Kathleen Potter, Allan Swift,
Helen J Wilson, Barry Woodward

DIRECTORS: Peter Boisseau, Bob Carlton, Terrence Daw,
Bruce MacDonald, Eszter Nordin, Nick Prosser, Richard Standeven

TRANSMISSION: January 1 – December 31

1985

HOUSE BY HOUSE

5 After giving birth to Claire at home in January, Sheila suffers depression. She is shocked when Bobby suggests having a vasectomy, but despite her refusal he goes ahead secretly. As a result, they discuss separation, but manage to resolve matters. However, an underlying tension would remain in the marriage. Later, Bobby is involved in strike action over redundancies at Petrochem, while Damon starts a YTS placement painting and decorating. Karen decides to do a degree in media studies at Liverpool University to be near her new boyfriend, David.

Filming Sue Johnston (Sheila Grant)

6 In August, Edna has a stroke and dies.

7 John Clarke turns up at the house blaming Sandra and Kate for the death of his mother in hospital. He holds all three tenants hostage, eventually releasing Pat and Sandra, but Kate ends up getting shot when she tries to stop Clarke killing himself. Pat and Sandra start a relationship; and when Terry moves in, he and Pat start a van hire business.

8 Paul is accused of bribery over the awarding of a maintenance contract. Annabelle starts a catering business from home. Gordon goes to live with Lucy in France in March, and Annabelle has a visit from the mother of one of his schoolfriends, who suspects that the boys have been having a homosexual relationship. Lucy returns from France in October for an interview for a translator, but is actually having an affair with a married man.

9 Heather has a relationship with her company chairman, Tom Curzon. He asks her to marry him in October, but she has reservations about him keeping his daughter's existence a secret from his family, and ultimately calls the wedding off. Heather later meets architect Nick Black after colliding with him in her car.

10 Tommy McArdle tries to warn off the 'Free George Jackson' campaigners. Terry and Michelle move in with Marie in February. After Little George is accidentally shot in the eye by an airgun pellet, George absconds from prison, only to be recaptured. Following more intimidation, Marie decides to sell the house and move to Leeds to be closer to George. Michelle joins her after she and Terry split up. In September, the Corkhills move in; and later Billy Corkhill crosses the picket line at Petrochem.

The siege begins

Sandra fears the worst

Kate fights back

Pat sees no way out

Taking a break – Sheila Grier (Sandra), David Easter (Pat), Robert Pugh (gunman John Clarke) and Sharon Rosita (Kate)

MERCHANDISE

For the first time, *Brookside* issued a calendar for the following year.

No.8 – The Collins' household

THE SIEGE

One event overshadowed everything else in Brookside Close this year. Having enjoyed success through the high-profile storylines with Petra Taylor and George Jackson, the programme was ready to bring real tension to the Close.

The Brookside Close siege saw John Clarke (played by Robert Pugh) hold nurses Kate Moses, Sandra Maghie and hospital porter Pat Hancock hostage in No.7, blaming them (unfairly) for the death of his elderly mother. The episodes that · unfolded were certainly gripping stuff. Francis Harcombe, who acted as Floor Manager during the story, remembered finding it both an immense challenge but also a great thrill to work on. Populating the Close with dozens of armed police officers marked out this storyline as something really spectacular.

Looking back, Harcombe has nothing but praise for Robert Pugh, whose performance was key to the story's impact. Similarly, a PA at the time recalls: 'Robert Pugh was absolutely riveting. In those days we used to have a rehearsal week prior to the shoot week. We would be relaxed, laughing and joking and then Bob would go into character and we would all be absolutely terrified.'

'FROM TRENDY CULT TO MASS POPULARITY'

While the on-screen characterisation and realisation of the siege were excellent, *Brookside's* motivation for running this story faced some questioning. While acknowledging that *Brookside* was now an undoubted success, the *NME* summed up its current status as being 'two remarkable stories: the rise of *Brookside's* viewing figures from trendy cult to mass

PLAYING 'THE GRANTS'

Ricky Tomlinson (Bobby Grant)

Born in Liverpool in 1939, Tomlinson had early hopes of a career in football, though this soon took second place to playing banjo in pubs and clubs across Liverpool. He went on to find employment as a plasterer, and in 1972 became involved in a builders' strike, helping to organise flying pickets. Refusing to testify in court against his fellow strikers, he was sentenced to two years in prison.

In 1982, he appeared in the BBC drama, *Boys from the Blackstuff*, before joining *Brookside* from the first episode. As Bobby Grant, Tomlinson provided not just *Brookside*, but British television, with one of its most overtly political characters.

Sue Johnston (Sheila Grant)

Born in 1943 in Warrington, Sue Johnston left school to work as a tax officer. Whilst still a teenager she had been fortunate enough to work as a secretary for Brian Epstein, and consequently had been close to *The Beatles* during their heyday.

Working at Pilkington Brothers in St Helens, Johnston launched the company's drama group and also worked in community theatre. Just prior to joining the cast of *Brookside,* she appeared in *Coronation Street* as bookie's wife, Mrs Chadwick.

As Sheila Grant, Johnston provided a stable and believable character, but one who would nonetheless go through substantial changes during her time in *Brookside*. So enduring has her presence been that she was invited back to reprise her character in the video spin-offs *Brookside: The Lost Weekend* and *Friday the 13th*.

Paul Usher (Barry Grant)

Born in Liverpool in 1961 and formerly a Bluecoat at Pontins, Paul Usher's first love was always music. Before accepting the role of Barry Grant, Usher had returned from a nine-month tour of America with the band *20/20*. He had prior television experience, having appeared in an episode of *Z Cars*, but when he answered Mersey Television's circular requesting new acting talent he was uncertain at first whether he wanted to stay in the business.

As Barry Grant, Usher provided *Brookside* with its first definitive 'scally'. The character went on to become widely popular, with the question, 'When's Barry coming back?' being a perennial query directed to the programme-makers by fans, so much so, that Channel Four had great success by trailing one of the 'returns' of the character in 1997 as 'Barry's Back!'.

Shelagh O'Hara (Karen Grant)

Shelagh O'Hara joined *Brookside* straight from school. She had been a member of the *Everyman Youth Theatre* in Liverpool, and it was staff at the venue, impressed with her acting skills, who indirectly prompted her to audition for *Brookside*.

Karen Grant's character helped foster *Brookside's* appeal with a younger audience. For perhaps the first time in British soap opera, hers was a character that pioneered the inclusion of teenage sub-cultures on British television.

Simon O'Brien (Damon Grant)

Simon O'Brien was born in 1965 in Garston, Liverpool. He was just starting his 'A' Levels when he landed the role of Damon. Although he had nursed ambitions of going on to university and pursuing a career as a botanist, his interest in acting took priority.

As Damon Grant, O'Brien was also instrumental in attracting the kind of young audience who traditionally did not watch continuing serials such as *Brookside*. His character's high-profile departure from the programme was a good reflection of how important Damon had been to *Brookside*.

Karen Grant

deal movingly with love in old age (as Harry recounted the struggles he and Edna had lived through). The fact that, despite being critically ill, a hospital bed could not be found for Edna prompted Conservative Central Office to complain that *Brookside* was accusing the Government of under-funding the NHS.

The birth of Bobby and Sheila Grant's daughter, Claire, also saw the programme explore another 'unsensational' topic: becoming a parent again in late-middle-age. This also indicated a sense of daring on *Brookside's* part in seeking to change the structure and composition of the family many saw as the programme's cornerstone (indeed, the Grant family were the only one featured on Channel Four's original on-screen promotional caption for *Brookside*). This move, however, was as good an indication as any that *Brookside* was not content to rest on its laurels and would continue developing its characters in order to keep the programme fresh. The arrival of the Corkhills in 1985 would build on that idea, and go on to provide the programme with its longest-serving character to date, Jimmy Corkhill.

REACTION

The 'siege' storyline created a media interest in *Brookside* that surpassed even the previous year's 'Free George Jackson' campaign. But did it elicit the sort of response the programme hoped for? Writing in *The Sun* in August, television critic Charles Catchpole was unconvinced: 'I thought *Brookside* was supposed to be about gritty reality. And I thought folks oop North were always popping in and out of each other's houses to borrow cups of sugar and the like. So how come the three siege victims were holed up in their home for FOUR days before anyone in the Close noticed?' When creating *Brookside* Phil Redmond had specifically stated that he wanted to reflect real life on a housing estate, of a kind where residents would not necessarily interact much at all and meet up over a pint to discuss their problems. Catchpole, it seems, was actually highlighting one of *Brookside's* distinctive qualities in his criticism.

In contrast, *The Daily Express* awarded 'full marks to *Brookside* for maximum claustrophobia', whilst *The News Of The World* on August 11 recorded that 'last week's climax to the gripping siege ended literally with a bang', continuing, 'if Brookside keeps this standard up the viewing figures can only increase.'

popularity, and the compromises, some scream sell out, that have accompanied and been the cause of that rise.'

For his part Redmond remained pragmatic, admitting that there was an element of audience grabbing at work, and that the episodes themselves received a mixed reaction. In the main it was felt viewers enjoyed the story, though some people thought it did not really represent what *Brookside* was supposed to be about. That it succeeded in boosting the ratings, however, is beyond question: eight million viewers, *Brookside's* biggest audience so far, tuned in to find out how the siege would be resolved.

DEVELOPING CHARACTERS

If the siege caused *Brookside* to be accused of pursuing the sensational, other storylines in 1985 provided something of a counter-balance. The death of Edna Cross saw the programme

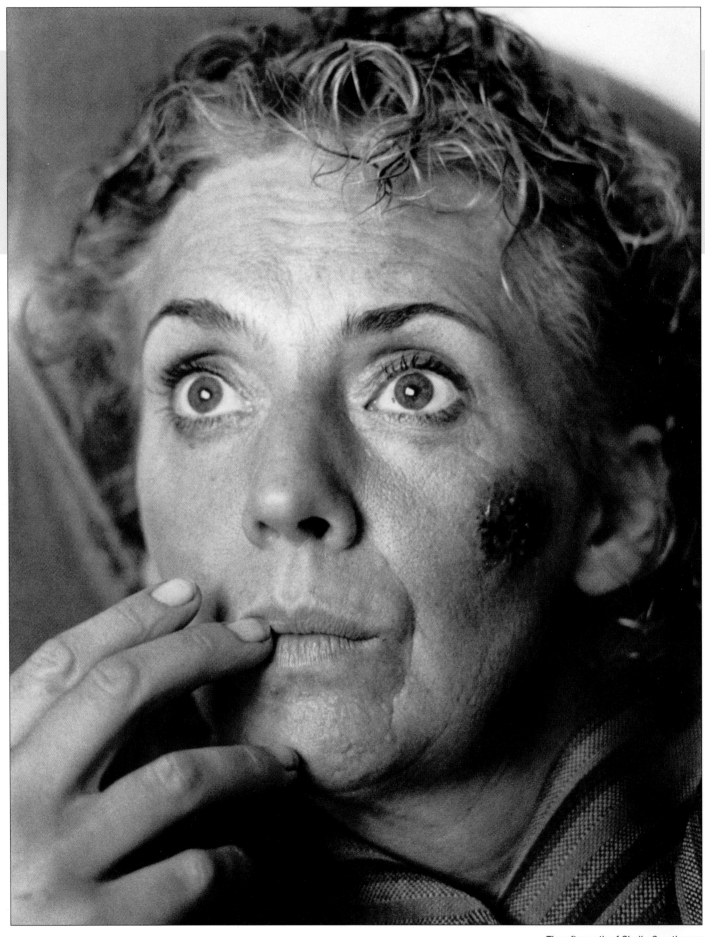

The aftermath of Sheila Grant's rape

BROOKSIDE: Episodes 333–436

WRITERS: Frank Cottrell Boyce, Andy Lynch, Alan McDonald, Jimmy McGovern, John Oakden, Jimmy Oakes, Jan Needle, Susan Pleat, Kathleen Potter, Allan Swift, Helen J Wilson, Barry Woodward

DIRECTORS: Peter Boisseau, Bob Carlton, Terrence Daw, Philip Draycott, Diarmuid Lawrence, Chris Lovett, Bruce MacDonald, Eszter Nordin, Nick Prosser, Patrick Tucker

TRANSMISSION: January 6 – December 30

1986

HOUSE BY HOUSE

5 Sheila's college tutor becomes steadily more obsessed with her, while her studies create tension between her and Bobby. Sheila is raped by a taxi driver and Matty is arrested, but released, only to find that his wife has committed suicide. Damon's YTS finishes, but he is devastated to learn that he will not be kept on in employment. He goes to Torquay in search of work and ends up sleeping rough. Karen loses her virginity to Guy.

Sheila falls apart

6 Harry places a personal ad, then feels disloyal to Edna. Ralph meets up with one respondent, Madge. Harry is delighted when his daughter-in-law Sally announces her pregnancy, but blames himself when the baby is born prematurely and dies after he and Sally have argued.

Harry seeks a new mate

7 Pat and Sandra grow further apart, and eventually she leaves in September with a new man. As a favour to McArdle, Pat and Terry accompany his mother to Barbados, but Terry is suspicious that she is actually couriering parcels.

8 Lucy's affair ends badly when she confronts her lover and his wife, only to be dumped. She goes to France with Barry Grant. Paul is made redundant in May. Gordon returns from France with a girl, only for Paul and Annabelle to find out she is his male lover's sister. Annabelle becomes a magistrate and gives up the catering business.

Billy and Jimmy's 'hot' bricks

9 Heather marries Nick in June. His friend, Charlie, tells her about Nick's heroin addiction. Nick overdoses, and his ex-wife advises Heather to leave him. Nick is sacked, then steals some of Heather's jewellery. Finally she asks him to leave in November, but he is later found dead on a park bench. Heather leaves the Close for Ireland.

Ralph Hardwick

10 Tracy Corkhill is having an affair with one of her teachers. Billy assaults him, and is convicted and sentenced to three months in prison. He wins an appeal, but is still sacked from his job. Billy's brother, Jimmy, appears on the scene with a load of 'hot' bricks, whilst Billy's son, Rod, announces that he wants to join the police. Billy is sacked from another job, leaving the family with severe money difficulties. Their utilities are cut off and the television is repossessed. Tracy starts a hairdressing YTS.

The Corkhills – Rod, Doreen, Billy and Tracy

THE CORKHILLS

The arrival of the Corkhills introduced another solidly working-class family to the Close – but as if to throw this into relief, the previous year had seen Billy Corkhill and Bobby Grant separated by a picket line.

On May 13, 1986, Jimmy Corkhill sauntered onto the Close for the first time. Initially only written in for six weeks, Dean Sullivan's portrayal of the character was considered so successful that he was invited to return to the programme full-time. Jimmy would quickly outgrow his role as 'Billy's scally brother' and become a well-rounded and popular character in his own right.

DAMON'S YTS COMES TO AN END

Unemployment had been a recurring theme in *Brookside* since it began, with both Paul Collins and Bobby Grant finding themselves out of work on various occasions. In Damon Grant's case, viewers had followed him through his latter years at school, and then watched him struggle to find a job upon leaving. In 1985, the Government introduced the YTS, designed to provide 16-year-olds with the experience and skills necessary to improve their chances of getting permanent employment.

In 1986, Damon was coming to the end of his YTS placement year and fully expected to be offered a job by the company. Instead, he was handed a glowing reference and told that the firm could not afford to keep him on as permanent staff. Devastated by this decision, Damon broke down sobbing in front of Sheila.

Barry Woodward, who wrote the episode remembers:

'The Saturday night that show went out, me and my wife, Anne, were at a party between Preston and Leyland. The woman who owned the house had invited her daughters and a bunch of friends back to the do after the pubs closed. They found out what I did for a living and when I admitted I'd written that episode shown earlier, things got really ugly. We had to leave, it was that heavy. Lots of the kids had suffered the same fate as Damon and their anger was channelled at me for sacking him. That showed me the power of popular drama with well-established characters and I believe we've caused a lot of discussion over the years. Incidentally, that YTS episode got ratings of eight million.'

This storyline was considered to be so rich that Vera Gottlieb, Professor of Drama at Goldsmith's College University, wrote a thesis on it for the book *British Television Drama in the 1980s* (published 1993). She described it as an example of 'the contemporary issue-led format which has made *Brookside* significantly different from traditional soaps'.

THE SOUTH BANK SHOW

On April 13, an episode of LWT's *The South Bank Show* was entirely devoted to the programme. This was the first real look behind the scenes at the making of *Brookside*. It began with presenter Melvyn Bragg on location being given a tour and a potted history of Brookside Close by Phil Redmond. The programme also featured a *Brookside* writers' meeting, with Producer Stuart Doughty chairing a discussion on how best to achieve the resolution of Damon's YTS storyline (this episode was scheduled to go out the day after *The South Bank Show* transmitted).

Particular time was given to comments from Jimmy McGovern, Kathleen Potter and Andy Lynch, with McGovern expressing his frustration that the production schedule did not allow the programme the flexibility to comment on current events. While he hoped that *Brookside* could come up with a mechanism whereby special episodes could be 'dropped in' at the last minute to remedy this, Potter sounded a note of caution, claiming that there was nothing so out-of-date as

'yesterday's issues'. Lynch, meanwhile, declared that he was proud that *Brookside* was seen in some quarters as 'left-wing', arguing it allowed discussion of matters that were otherwise kept out of the public arena.

Threaded throughout the whole programme were interviews with Liverpool residents with a variety of points of view; some felt that the Corkhills were unrealistic and that the programme was wrong to kill off its only black character at the time (Kate Moses) during the siege episodes, while others were of the opinion that *Brookside* was a positive reflection on Liverpool, and that it dealt realistically with issues of social relevance.

Redmond also reappeared, to answer questions from Bragg in a slightly combative but good-natured exchange, one of the questions being why *Brookside* did not deal with certain issues that were outside its scope... leading Redmond to answer (quite reasonably, even if mischievously) that this was because some issues were outside its scope! Bragg and *The South Bank Show's* conclusion came out in favour of *Brookside* and its innovative approach to drama.

Doreen and Billy

MERCHANDISE

1986 saw the release of two *Brookside* novelisations, *Brookside: Changed Lives* by Barry Woodward and *Brookside: Weathering the Storm* by Kathleen Potter, published by Methuen. These books were notable for being written by two of the programme's regular scriptwriters.

Some 16 years later, Barry Woodward still vividly recalls writing *Changed Lives* (which used the famous Brookside Close siege from the previous year's televised episodes as its basis). 'I finished it a few days before Christmas in 1985,' he says. 'It was written in 18 sessions, the last one lasting a solid 24 hours. Needless to say everyone wanted the manuscript yesterday. I slept for 20 hours after finishing it and couldn't go in my office for weeks without feeling sick.'

Alongside this, *Brookside* also issued a calendar for the following year.

BROOKSIDE TAKING ACTION: SOAP AID

When Sir Bob Geldof launched Band Aid in 1984 to kick-start people's consciousness on the famine in Ethiopia and raise money to feed its starving population, it kicked off a chain of similar fund-raising events and initiatives which included Live Aid the following year and, in 1986, Sport Aid and Soap Aid.

Featuring both pop stars and soap actors, Soap Aid was held at St Helen's rugby ground. *Brookside* (and at that time *Albion Market*) writer Andy Lynch and Tony Maher were the organisers, deciding to invite soap stars to the concert to give it its own unique identity. Because of Lynch's involvement, Mersey Television supported the event, with Ricky Tomlinson (Bobby Grant) acting as co-compere alongside a DJ from Liverpool's *Radio City FM*.

Headlining were Marillion, who had then just completed a successful UK tour. Other acts included Liverpool band, The Farm, and The Icicle Works, as well as performances by Albion Market's The Albion Market Band (who backed Helen Shapiro) and the cast of *Brookside*.

Steve Wright, Head of Music at Mersey Television, remembers: 'Paul Usher [Barry Grant in *Brookside*] wrote a song called 'Do it for the Children' and we recorded it at Strawberry Studios in Stockport where the original *Brookside* theme had been recorded. We got lots of artists to send in voice-over contributions for the song. We then had a couple of thousand cassettes run off and gave them away free at the concert.' Wright also remembers that a young musician who was keen to get involved was a then unknown Rick Astley.

Overall the day was judged a great success, raising thousands for famine relief.

THE RAPE OF SHEILA GRANT

The rape of Sheila Grant saw *Brookside* breaking more barriers with an unflinching portrayal of the aftermath of sexual assault. It also broke the dramatic 'code' of having awful events only befall characters that were either portrayed as victims or deserving of their own comeuppance. Sheila Grant was neither of these, and in fact for many she was *Brookside's* 'everywoman' – the moderate character with whom the audience most identified.

Her rape was shown as random and unexpected which added to its reality, as did the eventual unmasking of her assailant (a taxi driver whom neither Sheila nor the viewers had ever seen before). And while the actual act itself was played out off-screen, the aftermath on the character was depicted in commendable detail as we watched Sheila slowly try to rebuild her life. Sue Johnston rightly won numerous plaudits for her portrayal (the London magazine *City Limits* gave her the Best Actress award) as did *Brookside* itself.

When the rape episode was repeated in the regular omnibus edition (shown late afternoon the following Saturday) Channel Four decided to cut a shot where a coat was thrown over Sheila's head and she was dragged into the bushes – only for this act of censorship to receive three-times more complaints than the original transmission.

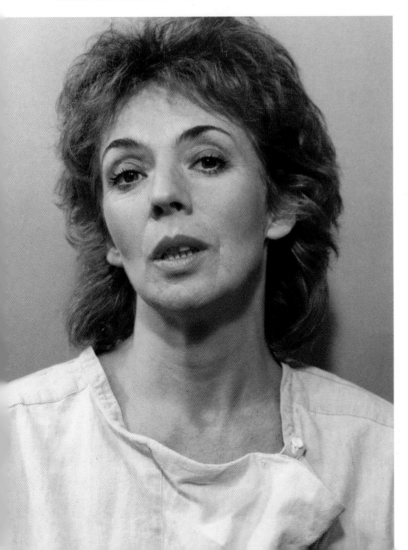

Sheila Grant

REACTION

Patently now one of the most trendy programmes on television, this year George Michael declared he'd like to have a part in *Brookside*. Initially planned to appear as part of the Soap Aid event, *Brookside* script writer Andy Lynch was quoted in the *Today* newspaper in May as saying, 'I am currently writing a script for George which would make him a member of the *Brookside* cast.' This, however, never transpired. Meanwhile, presenter of Channel Four's *The Tube*, Paula Yates, had actually succeeded in making it into the show, as she turned up to play herself presenting prizes to the winning floats in the Liverpool University Rag Week parade.

The programme was receiving more formal recognition too, being awarded the Judges Award from the Royal Television Society. As *The Daily Express* reported on May 23: 'Makers Merseyside [sic] Television and all those who contribute to the programme were praised for an outstanding effort by an independent company in setting up a long-running serial.'

'Melvyn Bragg bubbles over as *The South Bank Show's* Sunday night slot tunes in to TV soap operas,' declared *The Star* on April 17, signalling some rare interest from the tabloids in ITV's flagship arts programme. In *The Daily Mirror*, Peter Donnelly mused, 'Harry Cross must be Extremely Cross if he heard what Phil Redmond said on ITV's *South Bank Show*. "They're a kind of geriatric *Likely Lads*," said Redmond.' Donnelly then went on to quote Professor Laurie Taylor who also featured in the programme: '[*Brookside's*] not supposed to be a social documentary. It's a soap opera.' Donnelly then added his own endorsement: 'And a damn good one too.'

In mourning – Sheila Grant

BROOKSIDE: Episodes 437–540

WRITERS: Frank Cottrell Boyce, Peter Cox, Jim Hitchmough, Andy Lynch, Alan McDonald, Jimmy McGovern, John Oakden, Susan Pleat, Kathleen Potter, Allan Swift, Helen J Wilson, Val Windsor, Barry Woodward

DIRECTORS: David Attwood, Peter Boisseau, Darrol Blake, Bob Carlton, Terrence Daw, Philip Draycott, Ken Horn, Brian Lighthill, Chris Lovett, Bruce MacDonald, Alan Marsden, Eszter Nordin, Rob Rohrer, Richard Spence, Patrick Tucker

TRANSMISSION: January 5 – December 29

1987

HOUSE BY HOUSE

5 Karen moves to London, Barry disappears again, and Sheila and Bobby go to Rome to help get over the rape. Meanwhile Damon meets schoolgirl Debbie McGrath. Her father warns him off, and Damon's parents agree she is too young and as a result Mr McGrath sets Damon up with a job in Ipswich to get him out of the way. On his return, however, Damon finds out that Mr McGrath has been hitting Debbie. A fight ensues, and Damon and Debbie runaway together. Tragically, Damon is later stabbed and dies in York.

6 Ralph and Madge get engaged, but Harry exposes her as a gold-digger. He decides to sell No.7.

7 Terry's girlfriend, Vicki, moves in with him, but later moves out when he refuses to sever his failing partnership with Pat. Pat leaves when Harry gives him £500 to move on. When Terry also moves out in December, Harry re-lets the property to the Rogers.

8 Paul rescues a drowning puppy, Lucky, which Gordon and his friend, Chris, then run over in a stolen car. Paul blames Pat and Terry, and gets revenge by filming them working, and then shopping them to the DHSS. Annabelle is concerned about her mother, Mona, and brings her to live with them. Paul and Annabelle agree to find a care home to put her in, but when Mona visits for Christmas and claims the home are trying to kill her she is ignored.

9 Jonathan and Laura arrive, and drive into a large hole that has appeared in the road. Later they marry in August after one false start, but after a bodged DIY job on the electrics by her father, Laura is found in a coma. Jonathan invites Terry to move in with him when Harry gives him notice to quit. At Christmas, Terry chats up Jonathan's secretary, Sue Harper.

Paul and Pat look on

Bad news

Sheila at the window

Harry and Ralph

10 Rod starts Police College in January while Tracy is sacked from her YTS. Jimmy suggests a fake burglary to solve their money problems. He trashes their house, upsetting Billy's wife Doreen, and also burgles the Collins'. Doreen later finds the stolen property and realises it was a scam, but the building society start repossession proceedings. Billy breaks down when people start driving over his garden to get past the hole in the road. He drives around the Close over everyone's gardens.

Doreen

He resorts to crime to try to clear his debts, but the robbery goes badly wrong. Doreen leaves in November. Rod proposes to his girlfriend, Kirsty Brown, but she turns him down.

Debbie can't believe it

Billy has second thoughts

Billy 'The Driver'

HERE COME THE YUPPIES

1987 saw *Brookside* celebrate its fifth birthday, and the publication of the book *Phil Redmond's Brookside: The Official Companion*. It featured an introduction written by Redmond himself summing up the programme's achievements so far and signalling the way forward: 'In 1982, I wanted to tackle the relevant social issues. Things like long-term unemployment, women's position in society, the black economy, the micro-electronic technological revolution and its impact on both management and union structures within industry. Five years on, these issues are still a major concern to us, but the perspective has shifted slightly from the post-socialist society of the 1970s to the capitalist entrepreneurial ethic of the 1980s.'

When establishing *Brookside* back in 1982, Redmond had made the decision to set the programme on a private rather than a council estate, in part to reflect the increasingly higher percentage of owner-occupied homes in the UK (although, ironically, Liverpool still had one of the highest levels of council-owned property – but then, *Brookside* was never just about Liverpool, it just happened to be set there), and in part to allow him to mix different demographic groups within one environment.

The Collins family had reflected an affluence at the start of the decade (albeit affluence on the decline) while Roger and Heather Huntington portrayed an ambitious young couple with middle-class roots who were set on self-improvement – 'Yuppies' – before the term was invented. By the mid-eighties, however, an obsession with the 'enterprise culture' had prompted the media to coin the phrase 'Yuppie' and *Brookside* saw the arrival at No.9 of solicitors Jonathan Gordon-Davies and Laura Wright. Jonathan was a former public school boy from London whilst Laura had risen from a working-class background.

Their arrival in the programme confirmed *Brookside's* desire to feature a representation of the relatively young, well-off professional classes.

Brookside had always shown that its concerns did not remain just within the working classes. The death of heroin addict and architect Nicholas Black the previous year indicated the programme's willingness to explore challenging and dramatic storylines involving more affluent characters. In the case of Jonathan and Laura, Jonathan would have to cope with bereavement (Laura accidentally electrocuting herself in October 1987) and the following year, face difficult decisions about organ donorship.

Behind the scenes

THE HOLE IN THE CLOSE

There were more striking and significant moments created in *Brookside* this year, not least the appearance of a hole in the middle of the Close.

Creating the hole required a mammoth effort from the design department, as it was simply physically impractical to dig it in the middle of the Close. Shots looking into the hole were actually shots of another one dug in the back of one of the gardens. To achieve the effect of people descending into it required the use of a ladder with specially modified hinged segments. As the ladder was placed down into 'the hole' a member of the design department ensconced behind corrugated fencing on the constructed false wooden road would fold up each hinged section to give the effect of it disappearing downwards.

Right and below: Preparing the Close for the hole

45

Above: Boards are laid to make the hole
Below: Final preparations

BILLY REACHES BREAKING-POINT

In addition to providing a visual talking-point for the residents of Brookside Close – as they met up (normally on their way to the post-box) – the hole in the road also caused them to drive over Billy's lawn to get to and from their own homes. John McArdle, who played Billy, takes up the story: 'One of the most memorable scenes I ever did in *Brookside* was the aftermath of using Billy Corkhill's garden as a right of way for the Close. At the time, Corkhill was going through unemployment, he suspected his wife of having an affair with a dentist, his whole world – his whole family were falling down.'

Reaching breaking-point, Billy got in his car and drove round and round the Close, over all his neighbours' gardens. McArdle continues: 'It was a gift to get material like that and to be able to actually do it, because when I spoke to people in the street they were saying, 'I felt like that. You exorcised all my feelings on the screen because when you got in the car and drove round those gardens, you got everything out!"

'I remember one particular actor I've been working with recently and he'd just left RADA at the time and he said that a lot of the actors were out of work and they'd all come in and watch *Brookie* and that night saw me getting in that car and driving round and went, "Eh lads! Corkhill's gone mad! Get in here!"'

The scene neatly reflected the desperation of the character, who felt that having become a 'non-person' the whole Close could drive over his lawn because he was 'just a dole-ite'.

Ken Horn, who directed the episode remembers shooting this sequence: 'We used a scaffold tower for the master shot, then a hand-held shot from inside the car and a cutaway from inside the Gordon-Davies' house as it went past the window. John McArdle did all the driving himself, and the only notes I was able to give him on the scene was "do it quickly!" as we were running out of time. I'm chuffed that it's become so well-remembered, but the credit goes to John McArdle and Kate Fitzgerald (Doreen Corkhill) – they were terrific in their roles.'

Crane shot

DIRECTING BROOKSIDE: KEN HORN

Ken Horn was born in Durham in 1958. From Art College he joined Anglia Television as a trainee cameraman in 1978 and also went on to work for Yorkshire Television.

Horn applied for work on *Brookside* initially looking for the chance to become a Lighting Cameraman – a possibility offered by Mersey Television as Phil Redmond was specifically looking for younger talent (Horn was 25 at the time) to put in positions of responsibility normally only offered to persons with 20 years or more experience.

As a Lighting Cameraman, Horn worked on Brookside and Mersey Television's drama for Channel Four, *What Now?* In 1987, he became a Director on *Brookside* and also directed Mersey Television's *Waterfront Beat*. He left the company in 1989 to become a freelance Director with credits for *Emmerdale, Coronation Street, We Are Seven, Heartbeat, Boon, Casualty, London's Burning, Lovejoy, The Knock, In Suspicious Circumstances* and *Liverpool One*, plus, for Mersey Television, *And The Beat Goes On* and the first episode of *Hollyoaks*. Horn then became Producer for the BBC on *City Central*, and developed and produced *Mersey Beat*. He is currently working on a new ITV drama, *The Royal*.

Debbie and Sheila at Damon's funeral

DEATHS AND CAMEOS

The other significant event this year was the death of Damon Grant. Killed off in a special spin-off programme from *Brookside*, (generally referred to as a 'soap bubble') *Damon & Debbie*, it marked another turning point for the Grant family, and one that hastened their eventual break up. When it came to filming the scenes where Damon's body was brought home to rest things were not quite as they seemed. Unknown to anyone, Simon O'Brien (who played Damon) had crept onto the sets and, without warning, proceeded to bring Damon back to life again, to the shock of everyone.

This year also brought an unusual first for *Brookside*: a cameo by the Pope John Paul II. In March, the programme followed Bobby and Sheila to Rome. *Brookside* had to get special permission to film in the Vatican City and St Peter's Square, and to ensure the shoot ran smoothly, the crew had consulted a Liverpool priest before the visit. During the scenes in St Peter's Square, the Pope was clearly visible in the background waving to the crowd, and – some say – towards Bobby and Sheila too.

Sheila comforts Debbie

OUR LADY
OF
LOURDES

PRAY FOR THE SOUL OF
OUR BELOVED SON
DAMON GRANT
DIED TRAGICALLY
23 NOVEMBER 1987
AGED 19 YEARS

Sheila and Karen, laying flowers

POPE
Balcony spot in Brookside

By KEN IRWIN

THE Pope is to 'star' in the TV soap opera Brookside.

Producers of the Channel 4 show claim to have a TV scoop with exclusive film of Pope John Paul preaching from the balcony of the Vatican and TV stars Ricky Tomlinson and Sue Johnston

below in St. Peter's Square.

"The Pope made a surprise appearance on the balcony while we were filming in Rome," said a Brookside spokesman yesterday. "So this was a great bonus for

giving his Sunday blessing and benediction to the crowds, will now be featured for about three minutes in the programme to be screened on Easter Monday.

TV cameras were in Rome to film the happy reunion of Bobby Grant and his wife Sheila, who

Press report on the Pope's cameo

49

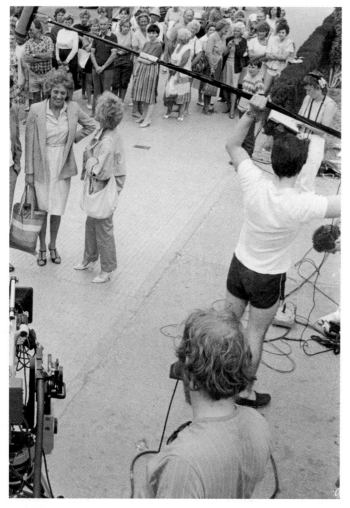

Filming Brookside

MERCHANDISE

Phil Redmond's Brookside: The Official Companion (George Weidenfeld & Nicolson Ltd) was the first publication to go behind the scenes, with a special introduction from Phil Redmond, and essays by John McCready examining the social context of the programme, the technology behind *Brookside*, the script-to-screen process and how location filming was undertaken, as well as detailing a house-by-house history of the Close and presenting biographies of the cast.

To coincide with the spin-off programme, *Damon & Debbie*, the closing theme, *Talk To Me* was issued as a 7" single. It sported two versions of the track, one subtitled *His Song* by Dani Ali and the other *Her Song* by Annabel Lamb.

Below: Behind the camera

Frank Rogers

Lucky and Annabelle

REACTION

The occasion of *Brookside's* (and Channel Four's) fifth birthday merited some retrospective pieces in the press. Most notable was the special supplement published by the television industry magazine, *Broadcast*. As part of various features celebrating Channel Four's anniversary, Phil Redmond was interviewed talking about what *Brookside* had achieved since 1982. He observed that since its creation, *Brookside* had 'accomplished much of what I set out to achieve dramatically. It has risen to and met many challenges. It has fought off much of the traditionalist thinking and forced other programme-makers to re-assess what they were doing.' Its success, meanwhile, was not because it based its plots in 'high drama', but 'more on the everyday, almost mundane things in life – and strong characterisations.'

Redmond also noted that by 1987, Mersey Television had created 120 full-time jobs on Merseyside with 95 percent of those people being local and the majority having never worked in television before. Asked what had been the biggest change in the programme over the five years, he chose the decision to drop all swearing from the programme.

The piece ended with Redmond's comment: 'We are, as *EastEnders* will become, a victim of the "familiarity factor". But keep watching. Changes are on the way!'

Christmas at the Collins' house

Damon & Debbie

DAMON & DEBBIE (3 x 60 minute episodes)

WRITER: Frank Cottrell Boyce

DIRECTOR: Bob Carlton

PRODUCER: Colin McKeown

TRANSMISSION: November 4 – 18, 1987, at 10pm

Opening titles

Debbie

Realising that Debbie's father disapproves of their relationship Damon Grant and Debbie McGrath run away together to York. There they squat in a houseboat (which they have renamed True Romance) and Damon takes up a job at a burger restaurant, Dick Turpin's.

Meanwhile, Mr McGrath is on the phone to the police haranguing them to find Debbie – but thanks to bogus postcards sent to him by Damon, he thinks she is in Margate. While Damon holds down his job, Debbie hopes to enrol at university in York and attends an open day where she makes friends with Jenny, an outrageous Goth who habitually attends such events to scam free food. Looking through Debbie's things, Mr McGrath finds a prospectus for York University and a note relating to the open day. His estranged wife arrives with her brothers Tone and Lonnie, who set off to look for Debbie – deciding to go to Margate 'via York'.

Whilst at work, Damon's boss, Lettuce, notices the owner of the houseboat has returned. Damon races him back to the boat but fails to get there first, and watches in horror as his 'home', complete with all his and Debbie's possessions, sails off. Convinced it is only a matter of time before the owner discovers their things on board and calls the police, Damon gets the bus to the university and tells Debbie they have to leave. Debbie is concerned that her diabetes kit is still on board, but as she has not told Damon about her condition she keeps quiet.

The couple go on the run to Bradford where they bump into Jenny and her boyfriend Kirk. Jenny offers to let Damon and Debbie stay with them. Kirk is working as a maintenance man on arcade games in the area, but hopes to impress his boss, Sadhir, with his own computer game.

Meanwhile, Tone and Lonnie arrive in York where they chance upon Dick Turpin's. Inside they ask for information about Debbie's whereabouts, but Lettuce misdirects them to Gretna Green.

In Bradford, Damon gets a job cleaning up at the football grounds. Kirk has managed to persuade Sadhir to come and look at his game, but Debbie inadvertently steals his thunder when she tells Sadhir's wife, Apala, about a computer game she has been working on based around romance. Damon is annoyed that Debbie has turned their relationship into a game and storms off to bed. Later on, he and Debbie row, and when he grabs her, her condition causes her to black out. Damon is scared, but Debbie refuses to tell him what happened when she comes round.

With tension high between the two couples, Kirk throws out Damon and Debbie, who then set off for Morecambe.

By this time, Tone and Lonnie have realised Lettuce misdirected them and so they return to the café and make her lead them to the university. There they are told that Debbie was seen with Jenny. Although they are unable to find her address, they do know she is connected to Kirk and they manage to track down his boss Sadhir. By this time Sadhir and Apala have taken in Damon and Debbie, and when Tone and Lonnie arrive asking where Kirk's house is, Sadhir directs them to it – the brothers unaware that Damon and Debbie were almost in their grasp.

The conversation is highbrow around the dinner table that night, but Damon is able to hold his own. Later on, Debbie tells Damon she wants to sleep with him, but he gets annoyed assuming she is only saying that because she feels guilty about being more intelligent than him. The couple argue and Damon runs off into the night. Meanwhile Tone and Lonnie are on their way back after being redirected by Kirk.

The following morning Damon returns and walks in on Debbie taking her insulin injection. Assuming she is a drug-addict he runs off distraught – and almost straight into Tone and Lonnie. Lonnie gives chase but is unsuccessful. Inside Debbie is becoming very ill – she thinks she may have overdosed. Tone puts her to bed and helps her come round with chocolate and a glucose drink.

Debbie explains her situation to the brothers who agree to take her side and help her find Damon. They follow him to York where he has started working for another themed café, Dunkirk's Marine Bunker, and Debbie explains to him that she is a diabetic. Damon is relieved.

After enjoying a Bhangra night in the city, the couple discover 'their' boat has returned. Going back to their home again, they stumble upon some thieves. As they make a break for it, one of them stabs Damon who collapses. Losing blood fast, he dies quickly in her arms, leaving her distraught and all alone.

'EVERYTHING'S BRILLIANT'

Damon & Debbie starts with a shot of the Liverpool skyline, familiar to 1987 viewers from the title sequence of *Brookside*, accompanied by a piano-based theme not entirely dissimilar to that of its parent programme. Innovative for various reasons, this spin-off from *Brookside* is best remembered for being the first of what Phil Redmond would dub 'soap bubbles' (because it 'floats away from the main soap' according to a November edition of *TV Times*). Taking place outside the normal confines of *Brookside*, *Damon & Debbie* was placed very carefully alongside 'regular' episodes of the series and portrayed a plot that ran parallel to the main programme. So in the same week Damon and Debbie were shown running away to York in their own series, their parents were shown fretting about their disappearance in *Brookside*.

Much as the opening title sequence suggested, this was *Brookside* – but at one step removed.

Watching *Damon & Debbie* is an interesting experience. Whilst it is an enjoyable drama in its own right it is almost equally interesting as a snapshot of an 'alternative' *Brookside*.

The drama employs some directorial and scripting flourishes that would seem out of place in the main programme; with cross-fades back and forth between sequences, Damon's thoughts made audible and dialogue at the end of one scene dovetailing into the start of another. An example of the latter comes when Damon tells Debbie: 'I'm just dead happy, that's all...' The word 'happy' is left to hang as we cut to the next scene and Tone's monologue as he is driving along with Lonnie (who, incidentally is played by Neil Caple who would join the *Brookside* cast in 2000 as Marty Murray): 'Happy. I feel happy. And it's the first time that the crunch is coming and everyone suddenly cheers up. It's like there's something in the air – everyone starts laughing and joking, but deep down inside you know that the crunch is coming. It's like the calm before the storm.'

It is also notable that dialogue such as this – which is effective but stylised – would not have sat well in *Brookside*. *Damon & Debbie* comes across as slightly more lyrical as a result, and suggests the serial was intent on carving out new ground, rather than simply staying within the conventional dramatic boundaries established by *Brookside*.

Filmed on location in York, Bradford and Morecambe, an additional consideration for the production was that Gillian Kearny (Debbie) was studying for her GCSEs at this time and so shooting had to be scheduled around her daily periods of study.

The death of Damon at the end of the three episodes remains probably the single most memorable moment from the whole serial. The viewers had been taken on a journey from a point where 'everything's brilliant' (according to Debbie) in episode one, to the death of a character they had followed for five years by the end of episode three.

At the time Simon O'Brien (Damon) confided in *TV Times* his reasons for leaving Damon behind: 'I'm whacked,' he said. 'I know people in the public eye are always complaining that they never get any privacy, that it's all go, go, go. Well, I'm not complaining because I wouldn't have missed the last five years for the world. But having said that, I'll be really pleased when I can go home for tea sometime, after working from eight in the morning until seven at night, sit down at the table and know the phone isn't going to ring.'

Wreaths were laid on O'Brien's doorstep by viewers the day after the final episode of the programme; a testament to the affection in which his character was held, and to the powerful quality of *Damon & Debbie*.

Ralph and Harry with Betty Hunt, campaigning

BROOKSIDE: Episodes 541–644 & New Year's Eve episode
WRITERS: David Angus, Frank Cottrell Boyce, Peter Cox,
Jim Hitchmough, Andy Lynch, Jimmy McGovern, John Oakden, Susan Pleat,
Kathleen Potter, Allan Swift, Helen J Wilson, Val Windsor, Barry Woodward

DIRECTORS: Romey Allison, Darrol Blake, Henry Foster, Tim Fywell,
Robert Gabriel, Ken Horn, Nick Laughland, Brian Lighthill, Brian Morgan,
Rob Rohrer, Richard Spence, Patrick Tucker

TRANSMISSION: January 4–December 30

1988

HOUSE BY HOUSE

5 Bobby is resentful of the amount of time Sheila is spending on her Open University course. He loses his licence on a drink-driving charge. Sheila hears that Debbie is pregnant and offers to help her raise the baby. She later visits a marriage guidance counsellor, but her marriage deteriorates further following a night out with Kathy Roach. Eventually Bobby leaves, and shortly after Sheila and Claire depart No.5 as well.

Paul and Annabelle

6 Harry puts No.7 up for sale. In December, he becomes a grandfather to Tim.

7 Geoff Rogers is skipping school, and there is no sign of the desk job Frank has been promised. The Rogers buy No.7 when Harry puts it up for sale.

Will Barry kill the dog?

8 Paul encourages Gordon to break from Christopher, who he feels is a bad influence on him. Mona continues to complain of her treatment at the home, and eventually runs away. An investigation finds that she was being abused. Paul is upset to find Gordon and Christopher are sleeping together in the house. Gordon and Chris are assaulted by 'queer-bashers', harassed by phone-calls, and the house is covered with graffiti. Paul eventually insists Christopher leave, and the couple later split. Annabelle has an affair with fellow magistrate Brian Lawrence, who gives Gordon a job in his car dealership, but Gordon soon finds out about their relationship. Paul discovers the affair at Christmas, and Annabelle leaves.

Christopher hides

9 Laura is declared brain-dead and her ventilator switched off. Jonathan lies at the inquest to spare her father from the knowledge he killed his daughter with his faulty wiring. Terry becomes a taxi driver. On a skiing trip, Jonathan meets Cheryl, a Canadian. He hooks up with her again on a business trip, and she later breaks with her fiancé to come back to England and move in with him. Sue and Terry get together in August while Jonathan is away in Canada, and are engaged in November.

Graffiti at No.8

55

Kathy, Sheila and Billy

10 Billy goes to Bristol to look for Doreen. Jimmy, his mistress Kathy Roach, and Tracy's boyfriend all move into the house. Jimmy persuades Billy to convert the garage into another bedroom. Jimmy goes back to his wife Jackie, and then Kathy moves out to make room for Sheila. Sheila and Billy kiss at New Year. Tracy gets a new job, but is sexually harassed by her boss at Christmas. Rod starts an affair with WPC Emma Reid.

Billy Corkhill

Billy and Sheila

The kiss

Sheila reflects

Harry, Sammy and Sheila advertising change in TV nights

Paul and Annabelle remove 'queer bashers' graffiti

DIFFICULT DECISIONS

1988 was to be about the break up of the Grants' marriage, but the year started with a moving storyline for Jonathan Gordon-Davies that saw him having to face the death of his wife Laura. Up until then she had been kept alive via an artificial ventilator; now the question of organ donation had to be addressed, leaving Jonathan and Laura's parents with a difficult decision.

Script-writer Peter Cox has commented that this was one of his own favourite episodes: 'I wrote in a non-speaking extra going by with a little blonde child. Suddenly the chance to give "the gift of life" became very real for them and this got a lot of strong responses [from the audience].'

By the middle of the year, the crisis in Bobby and Sheila's marriage was all too evident, and in a memorable scene that saw *Brookside* marry comedy with drama, Sheila and Kathy Roach return to the Corkhills' house from a night out, pursued by two men. Finding Billy asleep inside they tie a bow in his hair, only to have their pursuers start banging at the door. Awoken, Billy sees them off but attracts the ire of Bobby who

marches across the Close demanding to know what all the fuss is about. Surveying the scene, complete with Billy and his bow, Sheila bursts out laughing. Disgusted, Bobby hits her. The moment was shocking, changing the mood in an instant. As a gesture that displayed the poor state of the Grants' marriage, it was highly effective and marked something of a climax in the slow deterioration of what had previously been *Brookside's* most solid relationship.

BROOKSIDE AT 6pm?

In 1987, Channel Four's founding Chief Executive Jeremy Isaacs announced his resignation and left to become Managing Director of the Royal Opera House, Covent Garden. Michael Grade, most recently Director of Programmes at the BBC, replaced him. Famed for his shrewd scheduling skills, Grade raised the idea of moving *Brookside's* transmission time forward to 6pm to help the programme capture more teenage viewers. Ultimately the plan was abandoned, but Grade's keen interest in the programme did result in *Brookside's* first ever 'five-nighter', which began on Boxing

Sheila and Kathy prepare for a night out

Day and followed Sheila and Billy as they finally got together.

Its success led to further plans being formulated for *Brookside's* future...

GOING SOUTH

1988 saw a second *Brookside* 'soap bubble', *South*, a partly educational venture made in conjunction with Channel Four's schools' series, *The English Programme.* It followed Tracy Corkhill and her boyfriend Jamie as they ran away to London, and featured a cameo appearance from notable *Brookside* fan and ex-Smiths front man, Morrissey.

Also going south this year were the whole of the *Brookside* cast, in aid of the BBC's annual 'Children in Need' campaign. Their participation in this high-profile event, which involved recognisable and popular faces in music and television helping to raise money for children's charities, was confirmation that six years into its life, *Brookside* had become an institution.

BROOKSIDE TAKING ACTION: CHILDREN IN NEED

Head of Music at Mersey Television, Steve Wright, remembers that Steven Pinner, who played Jonathan Gordon-Davies (now Steven Finch), wrote a song for the event entitled *Let Them Know*. It was recorded at Revolution Studios (who let out their facilities free of charge in recognition of the charity) and produced by Wright. Soul singer and *Brookside* fan Ruby Turner contributed vocals to the track.

On the night of the *Children in Need* programme itself, the *Brookside* cast took a coach trip from Liverpool to London, stopping at every service station on the way down to busk for money for the charity. Wright recalls that John McArdle (Billy Corkhill) played harmonica, accompanied by Tony Scoggo (Matty Nolan), who played guitar and sang. In the meantime, Bill Dean (Harry Cross) went around collecting money from all and sundry – including those using the ladies' toilets! As the coach rolled south towards London, word spread and each time the cast stopped they were greeted by a bigger and louder reception.

Sheila puzzles over modern art

When they finally reached London, they headed for the BBC Television Centre and performed Pinner's song live on the programme, handing over all the money they had collected.

FROM THE ARCHERS TO BROOKSIDE

Back on the ranch, *Brookside* needed a new Producer. Vanessa Whitburn was working as a Senior Producer at BBC Pebble Mill in Birmingham, producing and directing a wide selection of plays for Radio 3 and 4 when Phil Redmond first contacted her. 'I think he had heard how much I enjoyed *Brookside* and what a terrific programme I thought it was from a colleague of mine in Pebble Mill,' Whitburn recalls. 'He was, as I later found out, on the look out for a Producer to run *Brookie*.'

After a series of meetings during 1988, Whitburn was invited to join *Brookside* as the Producer. 'I was delighted to accept,' she says. 'I learned a lot from Phil and I enjoyed my time there tremendously.'

In the seventies, Whitburn had been a Producer/Director on the long-running Radio 4 serial, *The Archers*. After leaving *Brookside* in 1990, the BBC invited her back to run the serial for a second time, where she has since gone on to further success and acclaim.

REACTION

Brookside's influence in popular culture was continuing to grow as icons of the programme turned up in peculiar places, none more so than Harry Cross' face embellishing – via the use of a terrible pun – the *NME's* weekly crossword.

Meanwhile, Phil Redmond was asked to contribute to the British Film Institute's 'One Day in the Life of Television' initiative, where both programme-makers and viewers were asked to submit a diary entry detailing exactly what programmes they had either watched or been involved in making on November 1. Redmond's journal included: 'At The *Manchester Evening News* Theatre Awards lunch I presented the best actress award to Josephine Blake and Diane Langton, and took the opportunity to make the point that Sue Johnston is one of the best actresses in the country…'

South

In London

On the tube

Tracy Corkhill

Jamie Henderson

SOUTH (2 x 30 minute episodes)

WRITER: Frank Cottrell Boyce

DIRECTOR: Peter Boisseau

PRODUCERS: Peter Griffiths and Phil Redmond

TRANSMISSION: March 14 – 21, 1988 at 10.33am

Deciding that there is no future for them in Liverpool, Tracy Corkhill and her boyfriend, Jamie Henderson, decide to head south to London where Jamie expects to pick up work at his friend Jazz's club.

On their arrival, Jamie is pick-pocketed, and when they show up at the address given for Jazz's club they discover it has been demolished. Searching out her home, they are turned away at the door by Jazz's ex-housemate Santa who tells them she ran off with the rent money.

Despondent, they wander around London until Tracy decides they are going to go back and force Santa to let them in. On their return they are met by Tracy Fitt and her baby. Feeling sorry for them, Fitt lets the pair have Jazz's old room. She tells them that the owner of the property has cut off some of the utilities to try and force them out.

The next morning, Tracy meets the third housemate, Louanne, who works as a 'Cat-o-gram'. Meanwhile, Jamie accompanies Santa to a job agency where they pick up a day's work washing dishes. He returns home tired and irritable.

Santa and Jamie are next assigned work on a building site, but when Santa ties too many lengths of wood to a cradle the pile tumbles out as it is being winched up. The foreman is furious and wants to know who is responsible for the accident. Jamie sticks up for Santa, but in doing so earns himself a reputation as a troublemaker.

The next day, Tracy accompanies Louanne on her 'Cat-o-gram' rounds, which includes calling in at *Capital Radio* where Tracy comes face to face with the singer, Morrissey. Meanwhile, Jamie and Santa are not having any luck at the job agency. Santa has a word with Vinny, who is handing out the jobs. Vinny tells him that that Jamie is the problem, so Santa immediately ditches him and accepts a job on his own.

Travelling around London with Louanne, Tracy glimpses the kind of glamorous lifestyle she wants. At a trendy pub she bumps into Jazz who gives her tickets for a party later that night. Meanwhile Jamie confronts Vinny who tells him he isn't going to get any work. He pays Jamie for the days he has worked and suggests he buys a ticket to take him back up to Liverpool.

In the evening, whilst the house is empty, the landlord arrives and throws everyone's belongings onto the pavement and boards up the property. Jamie tells Tracy that they have to leave for Liverpool, but she wants to go to the party. Eventually she agrees to accompany him and they board a train heading north. However, just before it leaves, Tracy tells Jamie she needs to go to the toilet. As the train moves off Jamie realises that Tracy has taken her bags and left. Helplessly he watches her on the platform as the train leaves for Liverpool. Tracy turns and makes her way back out into London.

'WE CAME HERE TO BE TOGETHER. IT'S DRIVING US APART'

South was made as a co-production with Thames Television and transmitted as part of Channel Four's schools' series *The English Programme* (whose title sequence precedes *South's* own). As such, *South* is quite a different proposition from *Damon & Debbie*.

Much of this is due to the production style. Unlike *Brookside*, *South* is shot on film, which takes away the raw and immediate quality suggested by videotape. Another marked difference is the proliferation of contemporary pop music. At this stage in its life, *Brookside* was only using music composed by Mersey Television's Head of Music, Steve Wright. In contrast, *South* features notable songs by *The Pet Shop Boys* and *Aztec Camera* amongst others.

The fact the actors' names precede the programme's title also signals *South* as being quite unlike its parent programme. With the additional use of slow motion and cross-fades, *South's* style is distinctive but the programme still used *Brookside's* directorial, acting and writing staff.

The script, again by Frank Cottrell Boyce, is less lyrical than *Damon & Debbie*, but still a highly quotable piece of work. Tracy and Jamie are both given dialogue that efficiently communicates the utter desperation of their situation. 'It's like we've been swallowed up!' declares Tracy at one stage, whilst Jamie concludes: 'We came here to be together. It's driving us apart.'

More in keeping with *Brookside* traditions was the cameo from a pop star celebrity – in this instance, ex-Smiths frontman, Morrissey. Talking to the *NME* on February 20, 1988, he amusingly described the nature of his part while previewing the programme: 'I can't act at all, which is very surprising. I can't be natural in front of the camera... I can't even be natural when I'm lying in the bath. I did one thing for a *Brookside* spin-off called *South*, which is about Tracy and Jamie. But it's compulsive non-viewing, essential kettle-on time. I just play, believe it or not, me... in the foyer of *Capital Radio* waiting to do some incredibly duff acting. It's so bad that you'll no doubt video it and show it to everybody! I believe it's being shown at the end of March. I'm in normal costume, whatever that means, and yes, I have three or four lines to say. I'm sure even those will be edited down to an eloquent nod!

As *Damon & Debbie* had done before, *South* ran in parallel with regular episodes of *Brookside*. Leading up to its transmission, the programme showed the Corkhills' house becoming increasingly overcrowded, prompting Tracy to make her break for London. Then in April, *Brookside* picked up where *South* left off, sending Rod and Jamie down to London in search of Tracy.

Although *South* did not manage to impact upon the public's consciousness to the degree *Damon & Debbie* had, this is no reflection on the quality of the producing, directing, acting or script. Instead, it is perhaps more to do with the fact that *South* was transmitted during the daytime (hardly a time to garner massive viewing figures) and alongside normal schools' programming schedules. Nonetheless *South* remains an often overlooked, but wholly worthwhile part of the *Brookside* stable.

Jamie and Tracy

Sheila and Billy

BROOKSIDE: Episodes 645–748
WRITERS: Frank Cottrell Boyce, Peter Cox, Chris Curry,
Catherine Hayes, Kay Mellor, John Oakden, Susan Pleat,
Kathleen Potter, Allan Swift, Helen J Wilson, Barry Woodward

DIRECTORS: Romey Allison, Henry Foster, Tim Fywell, Robert Gabriel,
Andrew Higgs, Ken Horn, Nick Laughland, Barry Letts,
Brian Morgan, Jeremy Silbertson, AJ Quinn, Garth Tucker

TRANSMISSION: January 2 – December 27

1989

HOUSE BY HOUSE

5 In May, the Rogers move in. Chrissy becomes a school governor, whilst Sammy and her boyfriend, Owen Daniels, are left in a coma after a car-crash. Sammy recovers but starts drinking heavily. Katie is bullied at school.

Barry and Sheila row

6 Harry's daughter-in-law, Sally, suffers from post-natal depression. Harry offers Kevin a generous endowment policy if the baby's name is changed from Haynes to Cross, but Kevin refuses. Harry is alarmed to find out that Edna's grave has been moved, together with half the cemetery. Mick Johnson moves in 'temporarily', but becomes permanent when Ralph moves to Las Vegas with his fiancée, Lana Costello.

Doreen returns

7 The Chois arrive. Michael Choi begins a relationship with Alison, but his father disapproves because she is not Chinese. Later he plans to move to America with Alison, who is considering taking up a job offer over there. Sinbad falls for Michael's sister, Caroline, but she does not feel the same way about him. In December, her ex-boyfriend, James Markham, arrives and proposes to her.

Sheila spurns Billy

8 Annabelle returns, and Gordon takes revenge by selling lots of Brian's expensive cars at very cheap prices. Mona and Gerald Fallon get married. A young offender called Louise turns up on Annabelle's doorstep. She takes her in, but later discovers Louise is being sexually abused by her brother.

9 Sue confides to Cheryl that she is pregnant but Terry is not the father. Cheryl wants to move out together with Jonathan, but when he prevaricates she moves to a flat in Manchester, although the relationship continues. Terry and Sue are married in August, and baby Daniel is born in September. Jonathan proposes to Cheryl in December, but she ends the relationship.

Harry snoops

The Chois arrive

Barry and Sheila fight

10 Tracy is offered a job move, but decides to pursue her tribunal, which she wins. Rod proposes to Kirsty again but continues to see Emma, only for Kirsty to find out on his 21st birthday, and the pair split up. Billy tells Sheila he loves her and they go to bed, only to be discovered by a furious Barry. Doreen returns and tries, unsuccessfully, to win Billy back. Sheila leaves when she finds out about Billy's criminal past, but Tracy helps reunite them.

'REALISTIC REALISM'

On screen, *Brookside* remained as gripping as ever, and – as always – infused with an interest in contemporary social issues. When Geoff Rogers was revealed to be suffering from dyslexia, the programme was able to open up a discussion on literacy – something Redmond had been intending to do since writing his initial submission for Channel Four. In later years, *Brookside* would return to this issue (through the characters of Diana Corkhill and later Niamh Musgrove) and in 1999, launch the 'Brookie Basics' adult literacy campaign to tie in with the Government's National Year of Reading initiative.

Another storyline based on real life issues was the year's most dramatic sequence: Sammy Rogers and Owen Daniel's car crash. Reflecting a prevalent concern of the time – joy-riding – *Brookside* decided to make clear the full consequences of such a crime by staging a spectacular car crash and an

Billy by himself

unflinching aftermath. Owen was paralysed as a result, and later the Home Office Minister at the time, Chris Patten, singled out the storyline for special praise. He described Owen's injuries as a 'good example of realistic realism' and footage of the car crash ultimately made its way into the Home Office's campaign to help publicise the dangers of joyriding.

Danny McCall, who played Owen, had previously worked in a centre for physically disabled adults; as such, he told *The Star* in December, he believed he was particularly well-equipped to empathise with his character.

CHANGES

Major changes were afoot for *Brookside* as it reached the end of the decade. The drama serial that had so defined the 1980s was looking forward to the next ten years. As ever, *Brookside* remained unafraid of ringing in the changes and at Christmas, the programme temporarily switched from two to three nights a week. Reports indicated that this was a pattern that would be adopted regularly; indeed, from summer 1990, the series was to run three times a week permanently. In the meantime, Redmond was making necessary preparations for the acquisition of new premises for Mersey Television. A closed college of further education in Childwall was to become the location for the new production base.

MOVING MERSEY TELEVISION

On November 7, the *Liverpool Daily Post* carried an article headlined 'Residents' joy as pub appeal fails'. Although ostensibly reporting the success of a pressure group in Liverpool's Childwall district in stopping an extension being built onto a local pub, it contained the following passage: 'Childwall conservationists are demanding an assurance from Liverpool City Council that a proposed television centre in the area will not disturb the environment... Mersey Television has applied for planning permission to turn part of the playing fields and buildings at Childwall College... into a television and film production centre. The "Friends of Childwall" group yesterday asked for more details of what they consider "ambiguous" plans...'

Billy Corkhill

REACTION

Responding to the rise of the younger characters in *Brookside* this year, it seemed that you could not open a teenage magazine without coming face to face with either Rachel Lindsay (Sammy) or Danny McCall (Owen). For some of the readers of *The Sunday Post*, however, this was a cause for concern. On December 10, the newspaper carried a letter from a Miss V Checkley of Manchester stating: 'Not nearly as good as it used to be. It was my favourite soap, but not since the young ones have taken over.' In response, the programme-makers were quoted as saying: 'If we didn't bring in youngsters, what would *Brookside* look like in 10 years?'

Finally, at Christmas, *Broadcast* magazine listed 'the broadcasting stars of the decade'. Amongst their number was Phil Redmond. The issue noted: 'He started off living in a garret and writing storylines for the "hilarious" *Doctor At Large*. But then brought us the spotty stars of *Grange Hill* and of course *Brookside* — the only soap on British telly to use the word "bollocks" — though it later contributed the much more famous phrase "fiddle the lekky".'

Terry tackles Sue about her infidelity

BROOKSIDE: Episodes 749–879
WRITERS: Joe Ainsworth, Maurice Bessman, Joe Boyle,
Frank Cottrell Boyce, Peter Cox, Chris Curry, Catherine Hayes,
Sam Jacobs, Andy Lynch, Susan Pleat, Kathleen Potter,
Allan Swift, Val Windsor, Barry Woodward

DIRECTORS: Celia Bannerman, Darrol Blake, Philip Casson,
Tim Fywell, Robert Gabriel, Andrew Higgs, Danny Hiller, Ken Horn,
Chris Johnston, Rita Leena Lynn, Barry Letts, Brian Morgan,
Betsan Morris Evans, John Strickland,
AJ Quinn, Patrick Tucker, Misha Williams

TRANSMISSION: January 1 – December 31

1990

The Parade under construction

HOUSE BY HOUSE

5 Chrissy mobilises the neighbours to protest against proposals for a parade of shops near the Close, but is unsuccessful. After being made redundant she gets a job as school secretary, much to her children's dismay. Owen recovers from his coma but is confined to a wheelchair. Sammy battles her drink problem, and by the end of the year is sober.

6 Harry Cross moves to St Helens and lets the bungalow to Mick, who has now been joined by his estranged wife, Josie. Mick catches a burglar trying to break into his children's bedroom and knocks him unconscious. He is shocked to find out he will be prosecuted for using 'undue force'.

Tracy Corkhill

67

7 Caroline finds out that James has run up huge gambling debts and has also been stealing from her jewellery business. Panicking, James flees in Caroline's car, but is killed in a road accident in Aberdeen, which the police suspect was murder. Caroline leaves Liverpool, shortly followed by Michael and Alison, who emigrate to America. In September, Max and Patricia Farnham move in, together with son, Thomas, and live-in nanny, Margaret Clemence.

Jimmy and Sinbad, fundraising

8 Lucy returns from France, but doesn't get on with Louise. Paul and Annabelle decide against adopting Louise, and move to the Lake District. When Lucy leaves for France once more, Gordon moves in with colleague Judith. The Dixons arrive in October, only to upset the Farnhams with their garden full of 'junk'.

Sue and Terry fight

9 Sue hopes to offset her guilt over Danny's paternity by trying to have a baby with Terry, but at the end of June, Terry finds he has a low sperm count and could not be Danny's father. He throws Sue and Danny out. However the distress caused by the death of Sue's mother brings them closer again, Terry stops the divorce proceedings, and ultimately asks Sue and Danny to come back. Jonathan moves to London and sells the house to Terry and Sue. Later, Barry Grant double-crosses Ricky and Kenny Fisher who kidnap Sue and Danny in retaliation, mistaking them for Barry's family. Barry negotiates their release, but ends up locked in a freezer on Christmas Day.

10 Bobby asks Sheila for a divorce. Sheila then finds out that he has had his vasectomy reversed and that his new girlfriend is pregnant. Sheila agrees to marry Billy, and reveals that Bobby is not Barry's real father. Tracy and Barry begin a relationship, but on learning she is pregnant, Tracy decides to have a termination, which devastates Barry and Sheila. Jimmy and Billy start a feud with Godden, the man who murdered their brother, Frankie. As the feud escalates, Billy, Sheila and Claire leave for Basingstoke. Rod meets Diana Spence, a pharmacy assistant, and they start going out – but he keeps his occupation secret.

Former Childwall College, prior to conversion to MTV's HQ

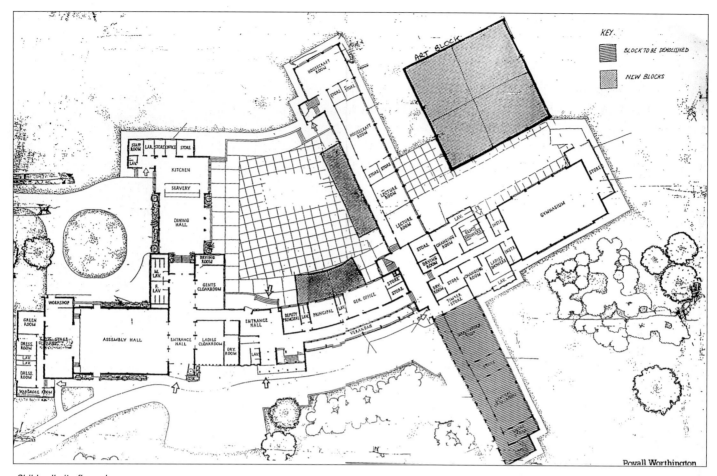

Childwall site floor plan

MOVING ON

Changes that had been promised in previous years came to fruition in 1990.

Mersey Television completed their deal with Liverpool City Council and moved to their new headquarters in Childwall. Surveying what was once a college, built in 1949, Phil Redmond realised the property offered some useful features. Because of its history, different sections of the property used varying kinds of brick, which gave the potential to make different scenes look like they had been shot in various different locations.

Mersey Television also continued to maintain a full production-base at the Close.

THREE NIGHTS A WEEK

The rationale for the move had been to prepare for *Brookside's* expansion from two to three episodes a week, which had come at the request of Channel Four's Chief Executive Michael Grade. So, from July 2, *Brookside* could be seen on Mondays, Wednesdays and Fridays. To help cope with

Ron and DD Dixon

the increased episode count, the programme took on a team of new directors, although the writing team remained pretty much unchanged. New characters also arrived in the shape of the Farnhams, followed shortly by the Dixons.

To heighten publicity for its move to three-nights, *Brookside* had made sure that it was running some of its strongest storylines over July, in particular, Terry Sullivan's discovery that Danny was not his son. Writer Peter Cox remembers: 'The toughest line I've ever written for *Brookie* was for Terry after he discovered Sue [had been unfaithful]. It was at the end of an all out row across the Close when he screams, "I hope you get AIDS!" at her. I know this caused a lot of consternation at the time [thanks to Channel Four's duty log of complaints received after the episode went out]. In reality it was early in the awareness-raising years about AIDS and I deliberately gave it to a character like Terry because it was very truthful for a lad like him to use such a non-PC approach.'

Brookside settled into its three-nightly schedule with great confidence.

MERCHANDISE

1990 marked *Brookside's* first foray into the home video market with the release of three volumes under the *Brookside Classics* banner by Video Collection International: *The Siege*, *The Sheila Grant Years* and *That Man Harry Cross*. Each tape contained three episodes selected to represent the given theme.

To tie-in with the video release, fans could also buy a souvenir T-shirt declaring 'Brookside Classics now on Video'.

This year also saw the publication of *Geoff's Story* (Walker Books). Subtitled *A case-study in dyslexia from Brookside* it represented the programme's first print initiative in providing support for dyslexia sufferers.

The Parade

CHANGING THE THEME

Brookside's theme music had always played a crucial part in defining the programme. From the outset, its synthesiser-based arrangement had marked it out as different from its contemporaries. To alter it for no good reason could have been seen as an act of vandalism. Nevertheless, Phil Redmond knew that to reflect changing broadcast technologies the theme needed to be converted from its original mono recording into stereo.

Mersey Television's Head of Music and co-creator of the *Brookside* theme, Steve Wright, takes up the story: 'We went down to Strawberry Studios in Stockport where the original theme had been recorded and tried mixing it into stereo. Playing it back, we felt that the synth now sounded a bit dull and flat and so it was at this stage we began playing around, trying to create a new version. I decided to update the sounds, just because technology had moved on since

MAKING MUSIC FOR BROOKSIDE: STEVE WRIGHT

Steve Wright was born in Liverpool in 1952. He went to school on Wirral where he developed an interest in music, playing in various bands and often performing his own material. Naturally he became caught up in the excitement of the burgeoning Merseybeat scene in the 1960s and left school, eventually becoming a much sought-after session musician.

He later moved from writing music for bands to composing television and radio commercials. In 1982, he secured the role of Head of Music at Mersey Television. As well as writing the majority of *Brookside's* incidental music over the last 20 years, he is also responsible for the *Brookside* theme, alongside Dave Roylance.

Wright has composed music for numerous other Mersey Television productions, including *Hollyoaks*, as well as co-writing (with Phil Redmond) a *Grange Hill* album and writing the music for the *Grange Hill* musical *Tucker's Return*. In addition, Wright produced *Let Them Know*, the song performed by the *Brookside* cast for the BBC's *Children in Need* programme in 1988.

Dave Roylance and I created the original and in some ways it did sound a bit dated, but I still kept it very faithful to the original – it's got the same tempo, for instance.'

Recalling the brief for penning the original closing theme music back in 1982, Wright reveals: 'The original end title theme was written specifically so that Directors could fade into the music at any point. So if the episode overran, they'd fade into the music at a later stage and make up the time with a shorter closing sequence.'

With the new version Wright comments that the tune we hear at the end of the programme can actually differ from episode to episode. 'Some Directors like to end on the drum-beats, for example, while others prefer to quietly fade the music in.'

The new music debuted on New Year's Eve and was generally well received, although Wright himself admits, 'you're on a hiding to nothing messing with something everyone knows.'

REACTION

Although *Brookside* had seen a recent influx of younger characters, it was to be one of the Close's senior citizens that spawned the programme's most notable crossover into the world of pop to date.

The Farm were a long-established Liverpool pop group now enjoying renewed fortune off the back of the 'baggy' movement from Manchester. Confirmed *Brookside* fans, they had a Top 40 hit with a cover of The Monkees' song *Stepping Stone*, and approached Rachel Lindsay (Sammy Rogers in *Brookside*) to appear in the video. Unfortunately contractual problems made this impossible, but for their follow-up single, *Groovy Train*, The Farm were successful in getting a *Brookside* actor on board: Bill Dean (Harry Cross).

The record went on to reach Number Six in the charts. Later, the band's drummer, Roy Boulter, would join *Brookside* as a scriptwriter.

The cross-over prompted the music press once more to sit up and take notice of *Brookside*, with the *NME* running a major feature on all the pop figures who had appeared in the programme so far, including Paula Yates, Morrissey (in the 'soap bubble' *South*) and The Housemartins, who had once visited the set and had their photograph taken with Simon O'Brien (Damon Grant).

Sue and baby Danny meet an assailant

BROOKSIDE: Episodes 880 – 1035

WRITERS: Joe Ainsworth, Maurice Bessman, Peter Cox,
Chris Curry, Andy Lynch, Mina Parisella, Susan Pleat,
Kathleen Potter, Allan Swift, Val Windsor, Barry Woodward

DIRECTORS: Darrol Blake, Danny Hiller, Jo Johnson, Chris Johnston,
Brian Morgan, Rita Leena Lynn, Brian Morgan, Jeff Naylor, AJ Quinn,
Allan Swift, Garth Tucker, Patrick Tucker, Misha Williams

TRANSMISSION: January 2 – December 30

1991

HOUSE BY HOUSE

5 Sammy returns from a hotel management course with 39-year-old Tim Derby. Following tension at home she moves in with him, only to be thrown out on her 18th birthday. Geoff's dreams are shattered when he discovers he will not be taken on by Tranmere Rovers – but later gets offered a YTS placement with Torquay United. Sammy has a reconciliation with Owen, and in October announces her pregnancy. Chrissy then leaves the Close in November during Sammy and Owen's wedding reception.

6 Against the advice of his solicitor, Mick elects to plead not guilty and face trial by jury, but is vindicated when he is cleared. Josie leaves him to go back to her previous boyfriend, Tony.

7 Patricia resents the re-appearance of Max's first wife Susannah, and following suspicions about his behaviour, throws him out on Christmas Day. Margaret and Father Derek O'Farrell, DD Dixon's younger brother, begin an illicit affair. Patricia finds a lump in her breast.

8 Ron puts his name down for one of the shops on the Parade, and The Trading Post opens in October. Ron's father, Cyril, is discovered to be a bigamist three times over, and later dies from a heart attack.

9 Terry is now fertile but Sue decides she doesn't want another baby after all. She introduces her friend from work, Fran Pearson, to Barry, and they have a relationship. Later, Sue meets Graeme Curtis at work, who quickly becomes obsessed by her. After she has sex with Barry, Sue feels guilty and decides she will try for a baby with Terry after all. But in October, pregnant, she and Danny are pushed to their death from scaffolding on the Parade. Graeme Curtis is charged with their deaths. In December, Terry and Barry leave and the Harrisons move in.

Max Farnham

Patricia, Max and Barry

Ron and DD

Sue and Danny

10 Rod tells Diana that he is really a policeman. Although angry, she later forgives him and they get engaged in May. Diana later confesses that she is illiterate; and when Rod is beaten up on his wedding day he leaves her stranded at the altar. Tracy goes out with Rod's colleague, Mark Potter, but in June he tries to rape her and she stabs him in the arm with her hairdressing scissors.

Sinnott leaps

Fall from scaffold

Danny and Sue

Mark attacks Tracy

THE PARADE

The increase in the number of Brookside episodes had brought about the need to create both new characters and new locations.

In January, work began on the Childwall site for the construction of what would become a major set – Brookside Parade. Designer Candida Boyes was assigned the task of reworking what had formerly been a science wing of the old college block into a modern shopping precinct. 'We couldn't

break the concrete skeleton of the building,' Boyes revealed, 'or we would have destroyed the structure, but we could break the bricks in-between. Wherever there was a window became a shop unit. If it was a big space, I partitioned it into smaller units. Work started on the conversion in January 1991 and we were filming there by July.'

In kitting out the different businesses, Boyes met with various challenges. Most of the food in Ron Dixon's shop was fake, with the designers trying to keep perishable products to

Sign to Brookside Close

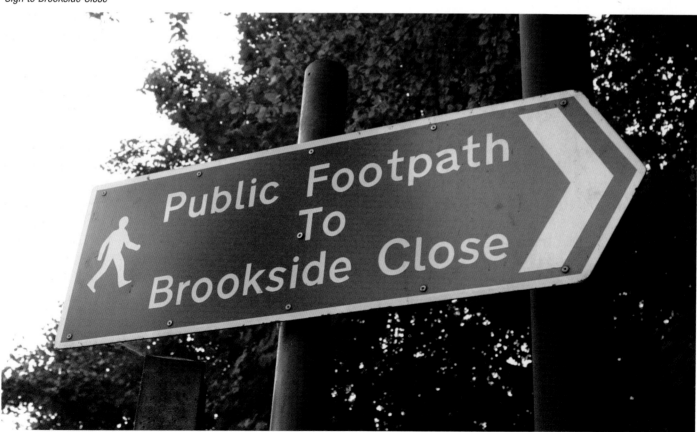

Recording Keith's drum music to be intercut with Sue's fall

a minimum. Real produce was used only if it needed to be handled by the cast. The freezer was never switched on as the buzz of the motors interfered with the sound, therefore all the packaging inside was actually empty. Meanwhile the hairdressing salon needed to be plumbed in, and the design of the Pizza Parlour required confirmation of whether or not the business made their own pizza bases. Once it was decided they did not, a stack of bases had to be acquired from a pizza produce wholesaler.

The on-screen opening of the Parade took place in October, but not before it became the subject of a police investigation...

EPISODE 1000

Long-running programmes love an anniversary, seizing upon it as a chance to lay on something really spectacular. Taking Annie Miles' (Sue Sullivan) decision to leave the programme as a starting-point, and realising that October would see *Brookside's* 1000th episode, Phil Redmond began to devise an especially memorable storyline for the occasion.

Associate Producer Mal Young was also thinking along similar lines and remembered: 'I wanted to get a big reaction from the viewers – I wanted something big to tie-in with episode 1000.'

At the long-term planning meeting that year Redmond and Young took the writing team through the proposed plot – Sue Sullivan was to be murdered. There was to be, however, a sting in the tale when they revealed that not only were they going to kill off Sue Sullivan, but baby Danny as well and Terry's child, which she would then be carrying. No other continuing serial had killed a baby before. The writers' initial reaction was that this was too grisly to contemplate – but Redmond and Young persisted with the idea.

Tragic end for Danny and Sue

'Only Phil and I knew who the murderer was going to be,' Young remembered. 'I didn't tell the actors because the minute you tell them, they play murderer in their eyes – they start playing sinister. I wanted them to play so innocent that viewers would think it was going to be someone else. The result was I had three actors banging on my door all year asking desperately, "Did I do it?"'

The writer of episode 1000 was Andy Lynch, who had a long history with the programme, writing the first ever episode not penned by Phil Redmond.

When it came to shooting the episodes, absolutely secrecy had to remain over who would push Sue and Danny from the Parade's scaffolding to their death. The three main suspects – Barry Grant, Terry Sullivan and Graeme Curtis – were carefully dressed in similar outfits as candid shots of part of the assailant were due to appear.

After using each of the three actors for various aspects of the scene no one, not even the Director, knew who was responsible for causing the deaths. Meanwhile, to shoot

Danny and Sue's fall, a low section of scaffolding was erected from which Annie Miles, holding a doll, jumped off onto a prepared mattress.

WRITING BROOKSIDE: ANDY LYNCH

Andy was born in July 1948 in St Helens, Merseyside. Upon leaving school he took up various clerical jobs and then worked in the chemical industry for about 14 years.

In the mid-seventies, he began writing radio-plays with some success but described it as a 'lucrative hobby rather than a wage earner.' He was recruited to Mersey Television in early 1982, after co-devising a television series for BBC1.

In addition to writing for *Brookside*, Lynch co-devised the soap opera *Albion Market* for Granada Television and has written for *Jury*, *Waterfront Beat*, *Emmerdale*, *Thief Takers* and *Hollyoaks*.

DD, Jacqui and Mike

Barbara Harrison

Graeme Curtis

REACTION

On the eve of the 1000th episode, *The Guardian* newspaper felt that: 'Recently... *Brookside* has been showing something of a revival by returning to what it is good at (violent, tragic, comic crime stories).' It went on to add, 'Typically *Brookie* is celebrating its 1000th episode by murdering one of its leading characters.'

Audience reaction to the deaths of Danny and Sue was huge. Piles of letters arrived from people who had recorded the murder scenes and scrutinised the pictures via freeze-frame. Some had resorted to counting the stitches on Barry's jeans and then comparing them with the stitches on Terry's.

Associate Producer Mal Young said: 'People counted the number of belt loops on the jeans, compared hairs on the arms, the types of denim, or analysed the tracks of the trainers as the shoe was raised in one shot. And having freeze-framed it, a lot of people magnified it, had a print taken off and sent me all the evidence!... It was exactly the reaction we had all hoped for.'

Terry plans his revenge on Barry

BROOKSIDE: Episodes 1036–1192
WRITERS: Joe Ainsworth, Maurice Bessman, Peter Cox,
Chris Curry, Shaun Duggan, Andy Lynch, Mina Parisella,
Susan Pleat, Kathleen Potter, Val Windsor, Barry Woodward

DIRECTORS: Darrol Blake, Sue Butterworth, Terry Green,
Danny Hiller, David Innes Edwards, Jo Johnson, Brian Morgan,
Jeff Naylor, Kay Patrick, Patrick Tucker, Claire Winyard

TRANSMISSION: January 1 – December 30

1992

HOUSE BY HOUSE

5 Sammy gives birth to Louise prematurely, in June. With Owen working long hours, Sammy can't cope, and abandons Louise outside the hospital maternity unit. Frank meets Lyn Matthews at her brother's funeral.

6 Mick loses his cab when his brother Ellis is caught driving it illegally. They decide to buy the Pizza Parlour from Terry, but Ellis borrows the money from a loan shark. The owner of the petrol station, George Webb, tries to petrol bomb the shop and Mick's house. Webb is eventually evicted from the garage, but threatens to harm Ellis' girlfriend Marianne Dwyer if they go to the police.

Sammy and baby

Patricia gets bad news

Max, dismayed

Explosion on the Parade

DD with Jacqui's friend, Leanne Powell

Terry on the beach

Barry on the beach

Julia Brogan

7 Patricia has breast cancer and has a mastectomy. She finds out she is pregnant, but later miscarries. Margaret and Derek set up home together when he leaves the priesthood. However when he leaves for Bosnia, Margaret returns to the Close. Max employs Anna Wolska as Thomas' new nanny. Diana Corkhill's arrival brings conflict with Anna, who is testifying for Peter in the rape trial. Patricia's father David Crosbie arrives.

8 Jacqui and her boyfriend break into the school, and she ends up trapped inside when he causes a fire. Barry Grant rescues her.

9 The Harrisons are investigated by Customs and Excise for VAT fraud, and get a bill for £70,000. John is arrested and cautioned for shoplifting. Their son, Peter, returns and gets a job at Petrochem. They leave in December, while the hate campaign against Peter continues, leaving him to face rape charges alone.

10 Jimmy takes advantage of Barry's absence to 'squat' in one of his shops. Gas cylinders in the shop explode when Barry sets fire to it to get Jimmy out. Diana and Rod are married in July. Rod is injured at work, and he quits the force. As their relationship deteriorates, Rod decides to move to Hull. Peter comforts Diana and things become intimate. Diana presses rape charges, but Peter claims it was consensual. The house is sold to the Shackletons and Tracy moves to Chester to manage a hairdressers. Diana moves into the Farnhams.

THE PARADE

Graeme Curtis is found guilty of Sue and Danny's death, and commits suicide. Fran leaves Liverpool, but returns when she discovers she's pregnant. Terry opens a Pizza Parlour on the Parade. Barry finds out that Matty Nolan is his real father. Barry tells Terry he slept with Sue, then hands him a shotgun. Terry doesn't shoot him – he wants Barry to suffer for the rest of his life. Barry goes to Spain, but returns later in the year, as co-owner of the Parade's new nightclub, La Luz, which opens on Christmas Day.

THE TENTH BIRTHDAY

The year brought another milestone for *Brookside* – its tenth anniversary. This was an undeniable testament to the programme's popularity, and proof that the continual development of format and characters had been successful in keeping *Brookside* both relevant and entertaining as audiences and television trends changed.

The publication of *Phil Redmond's Brookside: The Official Companion* in 1987 was followed in 1992 by a new *Brookside* book, *Phil Redmond's Brookside: The First Ten Years*. Once again, it contained a foreword from Redmond that mapped out how he saw the programme developing and progressing over the next few years: 'We have to reflect the changing society of the nineties. We've been through the strident eighties, what we're into now is the subtle nineties, where the marketing sell has got to be slightly softer because the audience are a bit fed up with the harsh kitchen-sink soap-box message. They say, "We know all that," so you have to put a different perspective on the whole thing. That's the challenge of doing a long-running serial – it's always the same but it's always different.'

If readers were inclined to interpret this as the end of *Brookside's* efforts to push back television boundaries, Redmond's closing remarks in his foreword showed that the programme still meant business: 'Our role, too, is not to let the Independent Television Commission become too cosy.

Every now and again our job is to shake the cage. I know at the end of the day that's what the public expect from us. They want *Brookside* to be challenging. And it will continue to be.'

Reflecting both Redmond's comments and the nature of the drama then unravelling on screen, *Brookside's* tenth anniversary found a programme that was arguably more character-led than ever before. Whilst it still boasted the strong social mandate with which it had become associated, it had moved on from the eighties subjects of union politics or unemployment, with issues and themes developed more organically from the characters and their lives.

DEALING WITH ISSUES

A case in point was Patricia Farnham. At the end of the previous year, she had argued with Max and thrown him out of the house. On her own, she now discovered that she had breast cancer, forcing her to re-evaluate her life and ask Max to come back.

While successful as a storyline in its own right, it also generated a large mailbag for the programme. Mal Young, who had now become Producer, revealed: 'The cancer organisations thanked us for highlighting it and a lot of individuals wrote to me to say how glad they were that we'd drawn people's attention to it.'

Ron Dixon comforts Jackie Corkhill

Setting up to shoot the scene with Barry and Terry on the beach

PRODUCING BROOKSIDE: MAL YOUNG

Mal Young was born in 1957, and before joining Mersey Television was employed as a window dresser for Littlewoods. At the same time, he was also playing in a band, an experience that drew him towards the entertainment field.

He started at Mersey Television providing three weeks cover as a Design Attendant, but ended up staying with the company. After a period working in design, he switched to become an Assistant Floor Manager at the suggestion of Phil Redmond. Young then moved on to become a Floor Manager, rising through the ranks to become Production Manager, then Associate Producer and finally Producer.

He claims he was given the Producer's job during a storyline meeting when Redmond left the room and didn't come back, leaving Young to finish up. Having proven himself, he was made Producer the following day. Young helped steer *Brookside* through its transition from two to three nights a week, and left the programme in 1996 to join Pearson, looking after *Family Affairs* at Channel Five. He has since gone from strength-to-strength as Controller of Drama Series at the BBC.

Nevertheless, there was a potential downside to dealing with issues that may have impacted upon the real life of a viewing audience. Young explained: '...some people thought we should have shown their version of the story. They said, "You got it wrong – I didn't react like that." ...I had to write back saying, "Sorry, but I can't feature thousands of people's individual stories." ...Not everyone who went through breast cancer was also going through the insecurity of worrying about her husband and his ex-wife, as Patricia was. She had a particular set of problems, and a particular set of reactions.'

The programme, as ever, took its public service responsibilities very seriously and Channel Four funded a special helpline for breast cancer sufferers, staffed by advisors and doctors.

GETTING THE FACTS RIGHT

Brookside's interest in depicting sometimes sensitive or controversial issues that may provoke strong responses from its viewers is one that demands the programme gets the facts right. With a topic such as breast cancer, for example, it is not acceptable to let the writers show any ignorance of the issue being discussed. The role of the researcher on *Brookside* has always been of considerable importance. *Brookside's* current researcher, Steve Byrne, reckons that whilst research is not the central element to storylining the programme, 'it's an important part of the process, but more of a supporting role.' He continues: 'It will tell you what you

can and can't do, and sometimes it may give the story a route not previously considered, but it's not central, and I think that's the way it should be. We're in the business of entertaining people, after all.'

As regards getting the facts right, particularly when the programme is covering sensitive issues, Byrne feels the responsibility strongly. 'You have to get information from the

Ron Dixon tackles racist George Webb

MERCHANDISE

Brookside's tenth anniversary brought another opportunity for readers to go behind the scenes on the programme. *Phil Redmond's Brookside: The First Ten Years* (Boxtree) was the first in a series of books penned by ex-ATV press officer, Geoff Tibballs. A lavishly illustrated volume, it invited us to 'Meet the Boss' (Phil Redmond, of course), while relating the story of *Brookside's* creation and examining how the programme develops from script to screen, as well as lifting the lid on the reality of Brookside Close.

In addition, *Brookside* also issued a range of commemorative merchandise, such as *Brookside: The First Ten Years* polo shirts and T-shirts, in addition to T-shirts sporting the programme's then current 'speech-bubble' advertising campaign.

Rather usefully, you could carry the lot home in a bag emblazoned with a legend boasting 'I've been shopping at Brookside Parade'!

postcards featuring posed photographs of the cast with dialogue and commentary presented in captions and speech-bubbles. Jacqui Dixon's increasing interest in the opposite sex was depicted in a poster showing a rather startled looking Ron and DD Dixon with the caption: 'JACQUI DIXON DISCOVERS HER SEXUALITY. UNFORTUNATELY, SO DO HER PARENTS'. Meanwhile, Jackie and Jimmy Corkhill's relationship was neatly summed up by the following exchange: '[Jackie] YOU LIE, YOU CHEAT AND YOU'RE PIG-HEADED, JIMMY CORKHILL. [Jimmy] SO, YOU'LL HAVE ME BACK THEN?'

John Harrison, shoplifting

REACTION

Brookside's more challenging stories this year prompted a variety of reactions. Praise for the priest Derek O'Farrell's affair with Margaret Clemence came from an unexpected quarter – the Catholic press were very complimentary about the priest's portrayal.

Meanwhile in November, the *TV Times* marked *Brookside's* tenth anniversary: 'Over the years, 124 actors have played main characters in *Brookside*. But Paul Usher as bad boy Barry Grant is the only original cast member left. "The years seem to have flown by," says Usher, 32. "It has been good fun, even though *Brookside* fans don't come up and talk to me any more. I think they're a bit frightened of Barry!"'

In *Brookside's* tenth birthday book, *Phil Redmond's Brookside: The First Ten Years*, the author Geoff Tibballs collated comments from some of *Brookside's* celebrity fans. Consequently we learned that writer and presenter Loyd Grossman had watched *Brookside* from the very first episode. 'One of the most appealing aspects of *Brookside* is the fact that we in the audience are living through the joys, sorrows and sometimes absurdities that make up real life,' he said.

Actress Pauline Quirke, however, liked *Brookside,* 'because of the comedy and also the way it deals with real issues.' Presenter Sarah Greene felt that the programme 'has the right balance in all respects – in its locations and in its light and shade between the serious issues and comic situations', but Michael Parkinson (whose son would appear in *Brookside* the following year as Susannah Farnham's lover) got the last word: 'Had it been set in Barnsley, it would have been perfect.'

horse's mouth,' he explains, 'from people who are living or dealing with whatever emotive subject it may be, every day. Their expectations are very high, they give up their time to speak to you, and make themselves available at odd hours, and so on, and you want to do them justice. I still find it difficult to watch the programme as a viewer – there's a huge sense of responsibility – not only to those interested parties, but also to colleagues. If something is wrong, it's a very public arena you may find yourself in.'

CELEBRATING THE ANNIVERSARY

To mark the historic tenth birthday, *Brookside* launched a special advertising campaign: 'BROOKSIDE – THE FIRST 10 YEARS'. Current storylines were reflected in witty posters and

Far left: Karyn Clarke; Left: Jo Halsall

Trevor Jordache

BROOKSIDE: Episodes 1193–1349

WRITERS: Joe Ainsworth, Maurice Bessman, Peter Cox, Chris Curry, Shaun Duggan, Andy Lynch, Susan Pleat, Kathleen Potter, Nick Saltrese, Allan Swift, Val Windsor, Barry Woodward

DIRECTORS: Sue Butterworth, Ken Horn, David Innes Edwards, Jo Johnson, Richard Kelly, Brian Lighthill, Brian Morgan, Jeff Naylor, David Penn, Nick Prosser, Beryl Richards, Jeremy Summers, Patrick Tucker, Claire Winyard

TRANSMISSION: January 1 – December 31

1993

Jimmy Corkhill high on drugs

Trevor

Frank crashes

HOUSE BY HOUSE

5 Lyn and Frank get married. On the way to the reception, Frank is driven off the road and killed by Jimmy Corkhill, who is high on cocaine. Lyn discovers she is pregnant, but loses the baby when she falls down the stairs. Katie turns to God, and Terry's new garage assistant, Simon Howe. She is initiated into his religious group by losing her virginity to him.

6 Ellis and Marianne's wedding is cancelled when Mick and Marianne realise their attraction for each other. As Mick's debts mount, he moves to the flat above the Pizza Parlour and the Crosbies move into the bungalow. David's brother, Clive Crosbie MP, commits suicide in his garage and his wife Penny comes to the Close.

Jimmy's horror

Lyn Rogers

Brian, Jimmy and drugs

7 Patricia sacks Anna who moves to the Harrisons'. Diana despairs at the 'not guilty' verdict in the rape trial, and slashes her wrists. Patricia's mother, Jean, arrives from Spain, and reveals that David had an affair with Patricia's nanny. Max starts an affair with Susannah, and so Patricia divorces Max. Following a late change of heart, the couple remarry.

Trevor attacks Mandy

8 Margaret and Derek go to Romania for charity work, but Margaret returns alone. DD opens a florists shop on the Parade and Ron starts an affair with Lyn's younger sister, Bev McLoughlin. Catching Ron and Bev kissing, DD suffers a breakdown and retreats to a convent. Tony Dixon is caught up in the car crash at the Rogers' wedding and falls into a coma. Bev starts a relationship with Mike. When she announces she is pregnant, Ron is sure the baby is his and asks Bev to move in. Josh is born on Christmas Day.

Beth Jordache

9 Peter is found not guilty of raping Diana. Anna tries to find an English husband to allow her to stay in the country and drifts into prostitution. Jimmy attacks Peter who decides to move to Oxford.

10 The Jordaches arrive, on the run from abusive husband Trevor. He soon succeeds in finding them and moves into the house, where the abuse resumes. Feeling they have no other option, Mandy and Beth kill him and bury him in the garden. Sinbad puts down a patio to hide the evidence. Trevor's sister Brenna reports him as missing to the police, and when Mandy is called in to identify a body, she claims it is Trevor's. Brenna wants Trevor's signet ring and so Beth has to exhume the corpse to retrieve it. Beth later sleeps with Peter Harrison, but ends the relationship when Jimmy tells her he is a rapist. Beth is attracted to Margaret and confesses her feelings at Christmas – but they are not reciprocated.

Sinbad and Beth

Tony Dixon

Frank Rogers

Simon Howe

Mandy Jordache

Trevor Jordache

THE PARADE

Terry helps Fran leave Liverpool. Barry's partner wants him out of the club, and frames him for attempting to murder Jimmy Corkhill, however his friend, Oscar Dean, is able to persuade Jimmy to withdraw his statement. Jimmy starts taking drugs in La Luz. He is later wracked

Beth, Mandy and Sinbad on the patio

with guilt over the car crash at the Rogers' wedding. Terry takes over the petrol station and offers to marry Anna, however Barry reports her to Immigration and she flees the country.

ENTER THE JORDACHES

One story would arguably go on to overshadow every other in *Brookside* this year, and earn the programme its highest viewing figures to date. 1993 was the year of the Jordaches.

The family arrived in February, but they were given a low-key entrance. Playing with viewers' natural curiosity at some more new residents, the Jordaches were initially kept off screen as other residents were shown wondering about who had bought No.10.

That their storyline was set to be sensational was something not lost on the programme's Producer, Mal Young, who felt that 'with the Jordaches, Phil Redmond probably came up with the biggest storyline in soap history.' Nevertheless, the production team were still to be

Jimmy Corkhill recovering from the crash

Mandy and Beth gaze at patio

overwhelmed by the public response. 'Even though it was controlled by us,' Young said, 'it took on a life of its own.'

Mindful of broadcasting restrictions, *Brookside* had to tackle the very difficult subject of sexual abuse with great subtlety. The programme took pains not to sensationalise either the abuse or the domestic violence on screen and filmed them as coldly and as blandly as possible. When Beth discovered Trevor in bed with Rachel the scene had to be constructed very thoughtfully, bearing in mind the fact that the episode was to be repeated at 5pm on a Saturday when children were likely to be watching alone. Therefore the

Trevor tracks down his family

Mandy and Trevor

Fran Pearson and baby Stephen

Sinbad with his mum, Ruth

programme showed Trevor cuddling Rachel (which could be construed to be innocent) and then getting into bed with her. The only real indication of what was actually happening was the look on Beth's face. In the weekday version, viewers saw Trevor's bare arm outside the bed, implying that he had taken his clothes off, but the shot was cut for the omnibus. In effect, it actually proved just as powerful because it creepily left more to the imagination.

Nevertheless, despite *Brookside's* caution, the programme still received a warning from the Independent Television Commission (ITC) over the knife scene where Trevor Jordache

PLAYING JIMMY CORKHILL: DEAN SULLIVAN

Dean Sullivan was born and educated in Liverpool. After gaining a B.Ed (Hons) Degree from Lancaster University he taught for several years in primary schools around Merseyside. He also took night-school drama classes for adults.

He made his professional acting debut at the *Pitlochery Festival Theatre* in Scotland, after which he toured in theatres all over the country, most notably at the *Liverpool Playhouse* where he was the lead in Phil Redmond's stage play, *Soaplights*. He joined *Brookside* full-time in 1990 (up till then he had still been working as a supply teacher). In 2001, Jimmy's 'own' website, *www.jimmycorkhill.com*, was launched.

was killed by his wife and daughter – despite the fact that viewers never saw the knife go in, or any trace of blood. The ITC's specific objection was to one brief shot of the instrument being dropped; their code of practice meant programme-makers were not supposed to show domestic implements as weapons before the 9pm watershed.

TURNING POINTS

In a year of dramatic stories, Jimmy Corkhill's drug abuse story was another high point.

The programme had tackled the subject before (notably the ground-breaking story with Nicholas Black in 1986), but never in such a raw manner. Although Jimmy Corkhill was always presented as a 'scally', he had retained a likeable streak. Now we were to see him descend into addiction and turning to crime purely to feed his habit. The storyline's initial climax, in which he caused the death of Frank Rogers and put Tony Dixon into a coma (which would end in his death), was shocking stuff.

Meanwhile Ron Dixon started an affair with Bev McLoughlin, and Katie Rogers was indoctrinated into a religious cult. All proved significant turning points in the lives of the characters.

LA LUZ

A subtle turning point in the life of *Brookside* had occurred at the end of 1992, when the residents of the Close finally got their own 'local'. La Luz opened on Christmas Day, 1992. Redmond believed it was unrealistic that *Brookside* characters should have a pub where they could 'announce all their private and personal business to all concerned' (as he put it back in 1987, in his introduction to *Phil Redmond's*

Bev leads Ron on

Ron restrains Bev from fighting with her sister, Lyn; Jacqui and Frank look on

Brookside: The Official Companion) and so the programme's only previous concession to a 'local' had been The Swan, which Jimmy Corkhill had been known to frequent.

The introduction of a club, however, came about because Redmond felt that the Britain of the nineties had become more affluent, and thought that *Brookside* ought to reflect this burgeoning 'café culture'.

While La Luz was a long way from being a typical pub, its metamorphosis into Bar Brookie in later years would provide the programme with its own meeting place.

Diana Corkhill and Peter Harrison

REACTION

The *TV Times*, which in January had been suggesting that Lisa Stansfield was set for an appearance in *Brookside*, carried a two-page preview of *Brookside's* 'Nasty Piece of Work', Trevor Jordache (as played by Bryan Murray), in March. 'While visiting a friend at the soap's Liverpool studios, he was introduced to producer Mal Young,' the article read. '"That's what Trevor Jordache should look like," Young announced, and promptly offered Murray the role.'

Mindful of the emotional impact the Jordache episodes could have on the viewer, Channel Four followed the long-standing policy of providing a helpline number after the programmes — something else *Brookside* had pioneered. In the first two nights after transmission, an estimated 260 people called. Meanwhile Anna Friel (Beth) received scores of letters from people who had been sexually abused.

Beth Jordache and Margaret Clemence

BROOKSIDE: Episodes 1350-1505
WRITERS: Joe Ainsworth, Maurice Bessman, Peter Cox,
Chris Curry, Shaun Duggan, Susan Pleat, Nick Saltrese,
Val Windsor, Barry Woodward

DIRECTORS: Jeremy Ancock, Darrol Blake, Audrey Cooke, Steve Finn,
Stephen Garwood, David Innes Edwards, Jo Johnson, Richard Kelly,
Jeff Naylor, Kay Patrick, Nick Prosser, Beryl Richards, Jeremy Summers,
Roger Tucker, Paul Wroblewski, Johnathan Young

TRANSMISSION: January 3 – December 30

1994

HOUSE BY HOUSE

5 The cult moves in. Simon pushes Katie too far and she moves out to the Dixons'. Barry buys the house and tries to evict them, but Simon barricades them in and takes Barry hostage. He then blows up the house, putting himself and Terry in hospital. After his release, he persuades Terry to join him in a suicide bid. Barry finds them and saves Terry's life, but leaves Simon to die.

Explosion in No.5

6 Penny finds out that her late husband had a long-term affair, and seeks solace in a relationship with Barry. David is judgemental about Beth and Margaret's relationship, and is shocked when Jean discloses that she had a female lover in her youth. The Crosbies live separate lives, and David has an affair with Audrey Manners.

Barry rescues Terry

7 Patricia finds out the baby she is carrying has Down's Syndrome. She and Max discuss termination, but decide against it. Alice is born in August, but Max has difficulty bonding with her.

8 A guilty Jimmy starts a fund for Tony Dixon, but dips into it to fund his drug habit. Tony dies in February, and Jimmy confesses at the funeral. DNA tests show that Josh is Mike's son, and a devastated Ron moves out of the house into the storeroom at the Trading Post. DD offers to make another go of things with Ron and they decide to renew their wedding vows. At the last minute, however, Ron returns to Bev, leaving DD devastated.

Max and Patricia

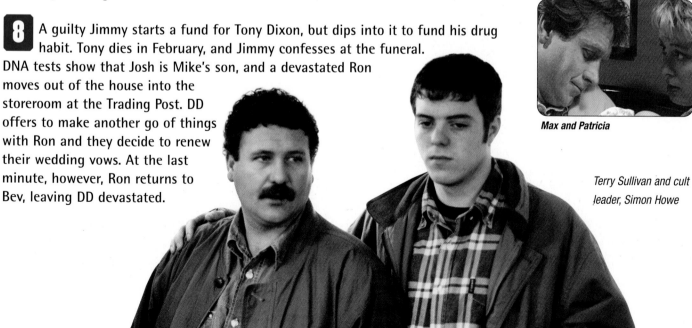

Terry Sullivan and cult leader, Simon Howe

95

Jimmy confesses

DD and Ron mourn

9 The Banks arrive, shortly followed by their son Carl, and his wife Sarah. Carl is arrested as an army deserter, but he wants out of the army and his marriage. The Banks' youngest son, Lee, is released from a secure unit where he has been held after crippling a girl in a joy-riding incident. With her family still seeking revenge, attacks escalate until a truce is finally called.

10 A cellmate of Trevor's turns up demanding money. Mandy gives him £700 from the Tony Dixon fund, although Sinbad borrows money from a loan shark to replace it. Margaret and Beth have a short-lived affair before Margaret returns to Bosnia with Derek. Mandy is upset when she finds out that Beth is a lesbian. With her debts escalating, her loan is taken over by Kenny Maguire who offers to accept 'payment in kind' from Mandy. Sinbad buys the house for Mandy, and unsuccessfully tries to pay off Maguire.

Jimmy ODs

Beth and Margaret

The kiss

Beth and Margaret enjoy a drink

THE PARADE

On the morning of Mick and Marianne's wedding day Mick is arrested for an armed robbery which was carried out by Greg Salter from the Pizza Parlour. Mick forces him to go to the police and confess. But it's too late for him and Marianne – she moves to Glasgow. Grants restaurant opens.

THE KISS

'Simon's at the end of his tether,' Lee Hartney (Simon in *Brookside*) told *TV Times* in 1994. 'Although he tries to seem cool, he knows he's on the road to nowhere. In desperation he's come up with the idea of a bomb.'

It would be a suitable metaphor for another explosive year in Brookside Close, a year that started with a kiss.

Beth Jordache and Margaret Clemence's kiss has since gone on to become an iconic image not just of *Brookside*, but also television drama in the nineties. But within the context of the storyline that had been running for some months beforehand, it was a largely unsensational – although important – event. *Brookside* itself had some awareness of how powerful the kiss might prove to be, purposely keeping details of it out of the press before transmission.

As the first overt lesbian kiss in any UK soap opera, it was undoubtedly a milestone of sorts, although it did provoke some complaint and the kiss was edited out of the omnibus repeat the following Saturday. In general, however, the programme was praised by gay and lesbian groups for its positive and non-clichéd portrayal of lesbians, and Beth and Margaret's story meant that 'the lipstick lesbian' was considered fashionable for a time in the mid-nineties.

In the long-term, the character of Beth Jordache was so well remembered that when Channel Four ran a poll of The 100 Greatest TV Characters of all time in May 2001, Beth was ranked at number 48.

Viv and Beth

'WE DON'T TAKE THE EASY OPTION'

In March, the Farnhams found themselves facing their own bombshell when Patricia discovered that the baby she was carrying would be born with Down's Syndrome. This was a sensitive story, which illustrated well *Brookside's* adeptness at dealing with difficult topics. The programme was tackling another contentious issue, but *Brookside* wanted to show that current medical technology allowed parents to find out at an early stage if a pregnancy was going to present any problems.

In researching Down's Syndrome, the programme found that many parents initially shun the child. *Brookside* was keen to confront this topic head on, with producer Mal Young commenting: 'When it was revealed that the baby would be born with Down's Syndrome, everyone expected us to have Patricia fall downstairs and suffer a miscarriage. They thought that would be our way out, but we don't take the easy option on *Brookside*. Instead we wanted to show the positive aspects of the situation.'

JIMMY'S STORY

Another long-term storyline took a further twist this year when Jimmy Corkhill, seeking money to buy more drugs, was imprisoned for burglary. Following his character into prison we saw him come to terms with being an addict, and make a decision as to what his future would entail once he got out. Jimmy's story had plenty of life in it yet...

Jimmy's lowest point

Simon threatens Barry

THE CULT

Whilst other storylines were developing over 1994, one came to a certain and spectacular full stop. The cult led by Simon Howe and based at No.5 Brookside Close had been established for six months, over that time indoctrinating Katie Rogers and then Terry Sullivan into their 'religion'. Now, however, things had reached a climax with Simon deciding to blow up the house.

This spectacular scene was achieved with air cannons in each of the bedrooms, and sugar glass in the balsa wood-framed windows. Smoke machines and a stack of paper placed in front of each of the air cannons completed the effect, which went off with such force that the roof of the house did visibly rise.

Barry gets his revenge

Terry, taken in by the cult

Simon prepares a bomb

SHOOTING BROOKSIDE

From the very beginning, *Brookside* has remained equally innovative in regard to the technology required to make the programme, as in the progressive plotting and characterisation it would employ over its 20 years. When the programme first started, it was shot on Sony BVP 330P cameras, which at that time were generally used on news programmes. Phil Redmond, however, had recognised that their comparative portability would be an advantage in navigating the unique set and location of Brookside Close. They did have their disadvantages, however, in particular producing a flared image if photographing a bright light source.

The programme then moved on to the Thomson 1657, an analogue camera that was convertible to digital format. This

in turn led on to full digital cameras and recorders. *Brookside* in 2002 shoots in wide-screen format (wide-screen being something the programme experimented with as early as 1988, according to former *Brookside* Director, Ken Horn).

Brookside also pioneered Steadicam in the UK. Ken Horn recalls that Redmond had been so impressed with its use in films such as *Rocky* that he had one imported from the USA at a cost of £22,000 – in 1985!

So successful was the use of Steadicam on *Brookside* that it would be five or six years into the programme's life before the production team used a dolly and track (the traditional means of shooting mobile camera action). Horn remembers a particular sequence in a 1983 episode that was wholly shot on Steadicam, following Bobby Grant through a factory.

MERCHANDISE

Phil Redmond's Brookside: Life in the Close (Boxtree) was another *Brookside* companion book. Again written by Geoff Tibballs, the volume focused on a house-by-house history of the Close.

1994 would in fact prove to be the busiest year yet in terms of *Brookside* publications. A special *Brookside* magazine was launched by The Magazine Company and sold around 35,000 copies and this year also saw the resumption of the *Brookside* novelisations, *The Journal of Beth Jordache* (Boxtree) by Rachel Braverman, marking the start of a series of novels to follow on in 1995.

Ron and DD grieve

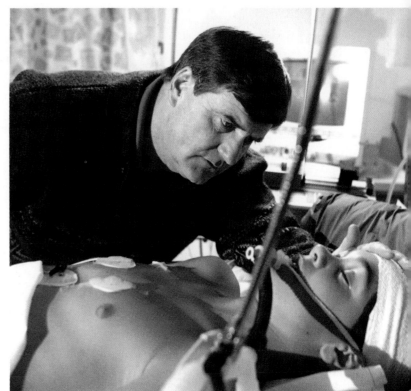

Ron at Tony's hospital bedside

pictures. Again, Mersey Television pioneered the use of this format, which gave more flexibility in post-production.

As for the future, it will not be long before *Brookside* switches over to solid-state digital storage, allowing the whole production process to be carried out on computer.

Redmond says he still gets a special buzz seeing Steadicam now being used at all major sports events. He remembers being told in 1985 that 'it was a film tool and couldn't work for video'.

Brookside started off being recorded onto one-inch composite magnetic tape, which had to be carefully laced onto huge reel-to-reel recording machines housed in a room separate from the vision gallery. Unfortunately, these tapes were subject to 'drop-out' and breaking, and the recording machines' heads frequently became clogged up.

Then came analogue recording formats in cassette form. Not only were these Beta and Beta SP tapes smaller, lighter and easier to use but they also produced better quality

Far left: Simon Howe; Left: Brenna Jordache

REACTION

The *Socialist Worker* magazine had an axe to grind: 'Producers of the Channel Four soap, *Brookside*, acted shamefully in dropping a lesbian kiss from the Saturday evening edition of the programme. They caved in to the anti-gay prejudice of the right wing press, despite the lesbian storyline "that has been running for a year" attracting just 14 complaints from five million viewers.'

Nevertheless, during the months when Beth and Margaret's affair was on screen, Friel was receiving more than 100 letters a week from viewers affected by the storyline.

Continuing *Brookside's* flirtation with pop-culture, Andrew Collins from *Q* magazine paid a visit to the Close and concluded that '*Brookie* towers head and shoulders above the competition because, within the twin straitjackets of soap format and commercial breaks... it creates powerful, funny, provocative – and, lately, gothic – adult drama.'

Top: Beth in her prison cell; Bottom: Sinbad arrives at court with Mandy and Beth

BROOKSIDE: Episodes 1506–1665
WRITERS: Joe Ainsworth, Maurice Bessman,
Roy Boulter, Peter Cox, Chris Curry, Shaun Duggan, Susan Pleat,
Julie Rutterford, Nick Saltrese, Val Windsor, Barry Woodward

DIRECTORS: Chris Bernard, Darrol Blake, Steven Bookbinder,
Sue Dunderdale, Steve Finn, Stephen Garwood, Jo Hallows,
Brian Lighthill, Cameron McAllister, Ric Mellis, Nick Prosser,
Julian Richards, Rupert Such, Jeremy Summers, Lou Wakefield,
Philip Wood, Jeremy Woolf, Paul Wroblewski, Johnathan Young

TRANSMISSION: January 3 – December 29

1995

HOUSE BY HOUSE

5 Carl and Sarah unsuccessfully try to make another go of their marriage. Carl takes a job in Dubai.

6 Audrey moves into the bungalow, and is shortly joined by her husband George, freshly returned from Kenya. Unknown to him, he is carrying a virus which sweeps across the Close, killing both him and Audrey as well as affecting several residents. Jean offers a home to Rachel, who is upset by Mandy's pregnancy. With their lottery winnings, Jean and David argue about where to go on holiday, and eventually go their separate ways.

Trial promotional material

7 Patricia takes over the florist, and it becomes The Gift Box. Susannah returns from the US and Max buys Barry out of Grants with money borrowed from David.

Trevor uncovered

8 DD sells the florists and leaves the Close. Bev moves in and the house is re-christened 'Casa Bevron'. Ron develops angina, and suffers a minor heart attack.

9 Rosie finds out she is pregnant, but loses the baby. During the resultant emergency operation, Eddie gives consent for the hospital to perform a hysterectomy. Rosie is furious and starts legal proceedings against the hospital. When the Banks' lottery syndicate with the Crosbies turns up a £100,000 win there is a dispute over the cash. Rosie becomes addicted to gambling, and loses the winnings, resorting to stealing from Grants restaurant to feed her habit.

Peter confronts Ron

Jenny Swift

Mick Johnson

Jenny's shrine

Christmas lights

Beth in court

Sinbad in court

Rachel, Sinbad, Mandy and Beth on the run

10 The patio causes water to flood the Banks' garden, who insist on digging it up. The Jordaches flee to Ireland where Rachel finds out what really happened to her father. They are apprehended and go to trial where Rachel denies that her father abused her, and Mandy (now pregnant by Sinbad) and Beth are found guilty. David Crosbie starts a campaign to 'Free The Jordache Two'. Rachel is persuaded to testify truthfully about her father, however Beth dies on the morning of the appeal from a genetic heart condition. Mandy is freed but Brenna secretly tries to poison her. Mandy gives birth to daughter Ruth in October and moves to Bristol to work in a refuge. Jimmy buys No.10, and the Corkhills move in. He starts a taxi business but it's actually a cover for drug dealing.

Rosie and Eddie

Julia's driving lesson

Rachel and Lee

THE PARADE

Leo's teacher, Jenny Swift, becomes obsessed with Mick who has to resort to legal action to keep her away. Becoming desperate, she threatens suicide, and then holds Mick at gunpoint. Finally she is sentenced to three years in prison. Mick and Sinbad decide to make a fresh start in No. 5. Jacqui opens Jacqui D's Style House with Peter Phelan, whilst Katie develops an eating disorder.

THE JORDACHE TRIAL

On screen, the year started with another five-nighter from January 30 to February 3 as the Jordaches fled to Ireland on the brink of Trevor's body being unearthed in the back garden. This story, which had been unfolding for two years now, was not set to abate...

The focal point became the trial of Mandy and Beth. In order to stage these scenes, *Brookside* decided to create its own permanent court set. An old props store was subsequently transformed into a convincing courtroom. The set is still used regularly by Mersey Television, and when not in use it doubles up as a rather grand meeting room.

In determining what verdict should be bestowed on Mandy and Beth, Phil Redmond took the decision very seriously. He told *The Liverpool Echo* at the time: 'The major theme was domestic violence and the legal definition of provocation when someone like Mandy, in an horrendous situation, strikes back and causes a fatal injury.' In deciding they would be found guilty of murder (although an alternative ending to the trial was shot in which Beth was acquitted whilst Mandy was convicted of manslaughter and sentenced to two years on a suspended sentence), Redmond wanted to reflect the fact that generally, if a woman kills a man, it is deemed premeditated murder because, in the

Patricia and Jackie support the Jordaches on TV

majority of cases, the woman has to plan how to achieve her objective. Redmond of course went for realism rather than following the popular feeling, which said that Mandy and Beth should be acquitted.

The day after the verdict was announced the charity, Refuge, was swamped with calls for help from women in similar situations. Sandra Horley, director of Refuge, said: 'Some were in floods of tears watching the programme. It was very lifelike.'

The production team on *Brookside* certainly felt that the trial had been successful in raising public awareness about this issue and were gratified when both the Metropolitan Police and the Home Office asked for copies of the programme tapes. The Metropolitan Police requested them to help train their officers dealing with domestic violence while the Home Office wanted to pass them on to probation officers having to deal with male offenders.

If there was any doubt about raising public awareness it was removed by the arrival of a news crew from NBC to interview the cast on the impact of the storyline, and its subsequent reporting in the USA!

Brookside's current researcher, Steve Byrne, started in that role around the time the Jordaches' appeal was being planned: Coming in on Mandy and Beth's Appeal was a bit of

PLAYING 'THE JORDACHES'

Sandra Maitland (Mandy Jordache)

In taking on the role of Mandy Jordache, Sandra Maitland found herself something of a figurehead for victims of domestic abuse. She would go on to become personally involved in support organisations and work in a women's shelter. Portraying Mandy, Maitland successfully conveyed both the character's strengths and weaknesses. It is a role with which she is still synonymous today.

Anna Friel (Beth Jordache)

Born in Rochdale in 1976, Anna Friel's initial ambition was to become a barrister until becoming interested in acting; one of her earliest television roles was an appearance in Alan Bleasdale's drama *GBH* in 1991. After an appearance in *Emmerdale* in 1992, she won the part of Beth Jordache in *Brookside*. Friel left *Brookside* in 1995 and has gone on to further success in films such as *The Land Girls*, *Rogue Trader* and *Me Without You*.

Tiffany Chapman (Rachel Jordache)

Born in 1979, the daughter of Huddersfield Town footballer Les Chapman, Tiffany Chapman was just 13 when she won the part of Rachel Jordache. Before joining *Brookside* she attended the Oldham Theatre Workshop. She still rates her early scenes as amongst the toughest she has ever been asked to perform on *Brookside*, but also feels she was too young to understand fully the implications of the storyline at the time.

MERCHANDISE

This year's video release, *Brookside: The Women* (Channel Four Video) brought together a mixture of current and past female cast members, alongside Phil Redmond, to talk about their experiences working on the programme. The result was an entertaining round-table discussion interspersed with archive footage. The same template was taken up for *Brookside: The Teenagers* (Channel Four Video) released later in 1995.

Meanwhile the *Brookside* novels continued going from strength to strength. *David Crosbie's Memoirs*, *The Jimmy Corkhill Story* and *Beth Jordache — The New Journals* (Boxtree) were all written by Rachel Braverman. The books were innovative in providing another 'layer' to the televised episodes, allowing us to be privy to thoughts and diaries that were not available to viewers.

1995 also saw the publication of *Sinbad's Scrapbook* (Boxtree), a large format book written by Frank Jeffrey with *Brookside's* Series Producer, Mal Young. Written from Sinbad's point of view, this was another lavishly illustrated book bringing us such insights as 'Sinbad's Scousespeak'. In addition, *The First Ten Years* was also revised and reissued as *Phil Redmond's Brookside: The Early Years*.

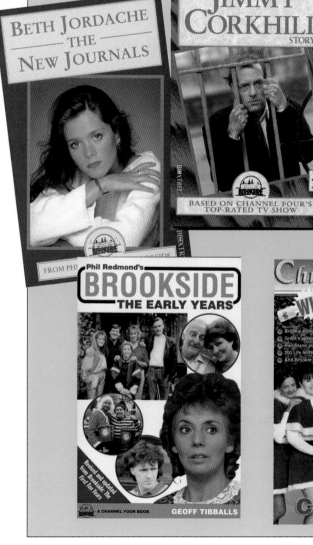

Jimmy's drug cover taxi scam

Cracker

the character once it became known that Friel wanted to leave. Redmond said: 'We couldn't leave Beth languishing unseen in jail because people would want to know what was happening to her,' he explained. 'Also Beth's death re-focused the story on Mandy's plight.'

HIGH DRAMA

In another example of *Brookside* reflecting current issues, the programme launched a new storyline in which Mick Johnson found himself stalked by Jenny Swift. The programme deliberately cast Kate Beckett as Jenny Swift because she looked so normal and innocent (in much the same way they had cast Bryan Murray against type as Trevor Jordache two years earlier), resulting in a mesmerising and memorable performance.

For another of 1995's major storylines, casting was again a key point, hooking the audience with a particular type of personality. The mysterious virus that resulted in the Close being quarantined and several characters being killed off stemmed from George Manners, who was played by veteran comic actor Brian Murphy. Murphy's casting encouraged the viewers, who would remember him as George Roper in the sitcom *George and Mildred*, to like the character and therefore be more affected by his death.

a baptism of fire. We had women's rights campaigners at the gates of the site after Mandy and Beth were jailed, and there was a huge amount of interest in the press because of the Sara Thornton case [Thornton had been controversially convicted of murder after killing her physically abusive husband]. Debate was raging about the use of self-defence and provocation as defence in murder trials by women who had suffered prolonged domestic violence.

The decision to kill off Beth drew some criticism from commentators, but it was felt that it was the best option for

REACTION

On all counts the Jordache trial could be said to have been a resounding success for *Brookside*. The storyline netted the programme its highest ever ratings to date, with roughly nine million people tuning in to find out how the case would be resolved.

While many of the television listings magazines splashed the Jordaches over their front covers, *The Liverpool Echo* went one better and published a special edition devoted solely to the trial. It was a mixture of fictional court reports and real-life interviews with the actors who played Mandy, Beth and Rachel, plus a piece talking to Phil Redmond. Sandra Maitland (Mandy) told *The Echo*: 'The scripts were a major part of the success. One minute the story was going one way and the next minute it was the other way.' She also added: 'I found it exhilarating in the courtroom. I think one cross-examination was something like 18 minutes.'

Further on in the year thoughts turned to the mysterious virus, with Phil Redmond revealing to *TV Times*: 'We're exploring how a community deals with this sort of virus. It reflects a basic fear within people — to step outside your front door and be struck down by a disease.'

Ron rescues Jackie after jealous Bev sets the house on fire

BROOKSIDE: Episodes 1666–1829
WRITERS: Joe Ainsworth, Maurice Bessman, Roy Boulter, Peter Cox,
James Doherty, Shaun Duggan, Helen East, Julie Jones, Julie Rutterford,
Nick Saltrese, Chris Webb, Val Windsor, Barry Woodward

DIRECTORS: Chris Bernard, Haldane Duncan, Sue Dunderdale,
Steve Finn, Maurice Hutchinson, Cameron McAllister,
Nick Prosser, David Richardson, Peter Rose, Rupert Such,
Jeremy Summers, Patrick Tucker, Lou Wakefield, Philip Wood

TRANSMISSION: January 2–December 31

1996

HOUSE BY HOUSE

5 Mick takes up bodybuilding and uses steroids, but stops when he realises that Leo and Gemma are frightened of his temper. Sinbad gets engaged to two women on the same day, while Mick meets a new girlfriend, Elaine Davies.

6 Jean decides to live in France and writes to David to tell him. Katie, Jacqui and Rachel move into the bungalow. Sammy appears, having left Owen, and she is drinking again. She goes to Tenerife and on her return is arrested for abandoning Louise. She is fined, and leaves the Close.

7 Max is wrongly accused of kerb crawling. Patricia refuses to believe him, so he moves in with Susannah. Patricia leaves for France. Susannah secretly buys Max out of the restaurant, but tells him he can have half of it back if they get remarried.

8 Mike is devastated to find out that Lindsey has gone back to Gary, after the drug trafficking charges are dropped. They are reunited, however, when she comes back to the Close, and they get engaged. Ron and Jackie come close to having an affair, and when Bev finds out, she sets fire to the house.

9 As Rosie and Eddie's relationship deteriorates, he has an affair with daughter-in-law Sarah. The building society start repossession proceedings and Rosie admits she has been gambling the mortgage money. After gambling away her compensation claim from the hospital they are left homeless. They leave the Close together to make a fresh start. The Simpsons move in. Nat marries his fiancée, but spends his wedding night with his sister Georgia, with whom he is having a secret affair. They are discovered by their brother Danny and so confess to their parents. Nat and Georgia move into the Pizza Parlour flat together, where Georgia discovers she is pregnant. Unknown to Nat she has an abortion.

Eddie Banks

Bev and Jackie fight

Bel Simpson, Ron and Jimmy

Julia with David Crosbie

10 Jimmy and son-in-law, Gary, import drugs, but are warned off by a local drugs baron, Big Davey, who riddles the house with bullets. Gary sells uncut heroin to Jacqui Dixon's boyfriend who dies as a result. Lindsey has an affair with Mike Dixon and they leave to go to Australia. Gary plants drugs in daughter Kylie's teddy bear and the pair are arrested in Bangkok. Jimmy persuades Gary to confess and Lindsey is released. Gary persuades her to come back to him, promising he will tell the police enough to get Mike released. Gary rapes Lindsey, and Jackie arranges for Big Davey to deal with him once and for all. Little Jimmy is in trouble with a gang in France who track him to the Close where they kill him.

Jimmy and Little Jimmy

Kylie's teddy bear

Kylie

Mike Dixon

Lee and Rosie Banks

Max and Susannah

In France

Nat and Georgia

Controversial relationship

CONTROVERSY

It was at a time when the Broadcasting Standards Council were claiming that viewers were becoming increasingly concerned about television companies pushing the levels of good taste in search of ratings that *Brookside* introduced perhaps its most controversial storyline to date.

In 1996, Phil Redmond decided to explore more pertinent questions in *Brookside*: What is this switch that occurs in puberty and adolescence which turns off the testosterone and oestrogen between brother and sister? At an age like adolescence, where anything with a pulse will do, why is it that you just hate your brother or sister? And what happens if it doesn't switch off? What happens then?'

Long-term *Brookside* writer Barry Woodward remembers the origin of what would become the Simpsons' incest storyline: 'The idea was first broached by [fellow *Brookside* writer] Joe

Ainsworth, and Phil Redmond was [initially] wary of it. I was interested in it because of some real life events I'd heard about in a village near my home.

'Originally, the story was planned for another family – the Banks, if I recall correctly. I can't remember why, but it ended up being transferred to the Simpsons.'

THE SIMPSONS ARRIVE

The Simpson family arrived in May, and by the following month, Nat and Georgia's incestuous relationship had been revealed. In retrospect, Redmond decided this had been a mistake, feeling that the family's initial 'big secret' should have been the sexual harassment case against the mother, Bel, by a young man at her previous job. Bringing Nat and Georgia's relationship to light so soon arguably meant that the viewers did not get to know the characters first – rather than viewing them as people Nat and Georgia almost became just a mouth-piece for the incest issue.

The programme received some criticism over aspects of the story. Some people felt that Nat and Georgia were too

Jackie, Jimmy and Lyndsey Corkhill mourn Little Jimmy

WRITING BROOKSIDE: BARRY WOODWARD

Barry Woodward was born in Everton, Liverpool in 1950. Leaving school, he worked for a print company before getting a job as a reporter on local newspapers covering the Huyton, Kirkby and St Helens areas.

As well as working as a reporter, Woodward did freelance work as an advertising copywriter. He also contributed short stories to a London magazine called *Ramp*, and wrote about a dozen un-produced stage and television plays. It was on the strength of one of these he was given a trial on *Brookside*.

Woodward's first *Brookside* script was written some months before the programme went on air, and was eventually transmitted as episode 22.

Still with the programme 20 years later, and with over 700 episodes credited to him, he has written more scripts for *Brookside* than anyone else.

As well as writing for *Brookside*, Woodward continues to do occasional newspaper and magazine work. He's also written for *Emmerdale*, *Heartbeat*, *The Bill* and *In Suspicious Circumstances*.

In addition to all his other work, Woodward wrote the second-ever *Brookside* novel, *Changed Lives,* back in 1986.

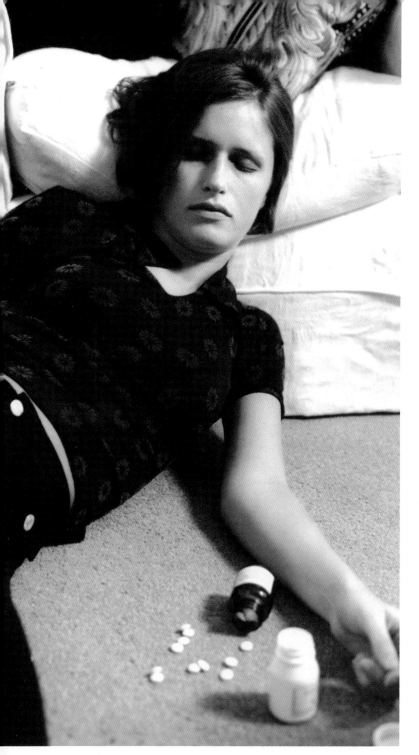

It's all too much for Jules Simpson

good looking, but in response Redmond felt that this was 'cultural naivety'. He had made the decision that they had to be equally attractive, and that Georgia was to be older than Nat so that there was no hint of coercion in the relationship. Coming relatively soon after the Jordache storyline, *Brookside* found that people were unclear of the difference between consensual incest and sexual abuse.

Top right: Jackie and Ron in Blackpool
Right: Fee Phelan gets her revenge on two-timing Sinbad

More fuel was added to the flames when Channel Four was ordered by the Broadcasting Standards Council and the Independent Television Commission to broadcast an apology about showing brother and sister in bed during the Saturday omnibus edition (which transmitted at 5pm, earlier than the weeknight episodes). Channel Four's statement read: 'We fully accept the ITC's judgement that the scene should not have been shown at 5pm in the omnibus edition. We are pleased that they recognise that this storyline was an appropriate subject for the 8pm weekday showing, in *Brookside's* tradition of dealing with important and difficult issues.'

Although the Simpsons' relationship drew flak to *Brookside* it remained a storyline that the programme could be proud of, so much so that when *Brookside* launched a second magazine in the summer, Nat and Georgia were the front cover stars.

MIKE AND LINDSEY IN THAILAND

Another memorable storyline this year saw Lindsey and Mike arrested for drug trafficking in Thailand. In realising the story, the on-screen *Brookside* production team faced a challenge in

Tim 'Tinhead' O'Leary confronts Sinbad

Hollyoaks meets Brookside – Kurt and Ruth Benson, Jacqui and Katie

Tinhead thinks about joining up

recreating a Thai airport. After exhausting all the obvious avenues in trying to find an image of the airport – aviation and architecture magazines and various affiliated organisations – a direct approach was all that was left. The team sent off a letter on spec to the Airport Manager in Thailand in October 1995, although they did not hold out much hope of getting a reply. However, as shooting of the episodes approached, photographs, newsletters and brochures arrived courtesy of the Managing Director of the Airport Authority of Thailand. Later in 1996, the team also received a greeting card from the new Airport Manager to commemorate the King of Thailand's golden jubilee!

Commenting on the story for the 2000 *Brookside* documentary, *18 Years Young,* Paul Byatt (Mike Dixon) said: '[The prison scenes] were good scenes to do... It was a good storyline. The only problem with it was I was out [of the programme]. I was in jail for four months!'

MERCHANDISE

1996 brought about another *Brookside* magazine, this time published by Attic Futura. Unlike their predecessor – the *Brookside* magazine in 1994, published by The Magazine Company – Attic Futura would go on to produce several issues on a quarterly basis.

Meanwhile, Geoff Tibballs had another book out: *The Brookside Files* (Boxtree) (which had originally been given the title *The Brookside Survival Guide*) was a mixture of 'first-hand' testimony from the programme's characters based around themes such as health and crime, and statements from Mal Young explaining why the programme chose to cover such topics.

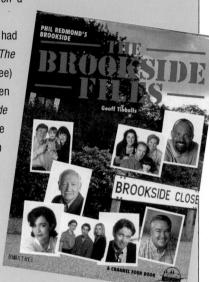

REACTION

'*Brookside's* incest storyline is its most contentious yet,' said *The New Statesman* on December 6. With Channel Four still under fire from the press (*The Daily Mail* infamously dubbing the channel's Chief Executive 'pornographer-in-chief'), *Brookside's* decision to take this moment to 'remind people that it is extremely difficult to predict, prescribe or legislate for the complexity of sexual relationships' (as Redmond told *The New Statesman*) was a courageous one.

Unsurprisingly, sections of the press were quick to denounce the plot. In response Redmond said: 'From the comments, you would think that we hadn't thought about all of this quite carefully. We wanted the characters to be attractive and it was important that the family should be perceived as both educated and intelligent, so that there would be no suggestion that the situation had arisen through ignorance.'

Proving that the programme was successful in provoking discussion about the issues it dealt with, *The Independent on Sunday* ran a thoughtful feature on consensual incest entitled 'INCEST: THE PSYCHOLOGY, THE LAW AND THE MEDIA' on December 11.

Sarah Banks and Mike Dixon

Jimmy Corkhill in the news

BROOKSIDE: Episodes 1830–1992
WRITERS: Joe Ainsworth, Maurice Bessman, Roy Boulter, Peter Cox,
Shaun Duggan, Julie Jones, Sue Mooney, Barbara Phillips,
Julie Rutterford, Nick Saltrese, Mike Stott, Chris Webb,
Val Windsor, Barry Woodward

DIRECTORS: Paul Annett, Chris Bernard, Jon East, Steve Finn,
Steve Garwood, Maurice Hutchinson, Chris Johnson, Dominic Keavey,
Jeff Naylor, Peter Rose, Rupert Such, Jeremy Summers,
Bob Thomson, Sue Sutton Mayo, Patrick Tucker

TRANSMISSION: January 1 – December 31

1997

HOUSE BY HOUSE

5 Mick proposes to Elaine, who accepts, insisting her mother Gladys – who is waiting for a hip replacement operation – also moves in. As a result, Sinbad moves out into the Corkhill's garage extension. Before she has her operation, Gladys finds out she has terminal cancer and asks Mick and Elaine to bring the wedding forward. She decides not to have any treatment, and makes a living will to stop Elaine or her sister Cassie sending her to hospital. Gladys deteriorates, and eventually, in agony, attempts to smother herself. Mick and Elaine help and they are arrested for murder. When Elaine goes on the run Mick changes his story, putting the blame on her.

Surprise for Jimmy

6 David takes over the petrol station franchise. Jacqui manages Bar Brookie (the replacement for La Luz) and is so successful she is offered a partnership. Rachel marries Christian Wright, who becomes increasingly controlling and abusive, before she eventually fights back. Jacqui has problems with a protection racket at the club, and pays Barry Grant to sort it for her, permanently.

Barry Grant's back

7 Matthew and Emily are killed in a car crash. Susannah blames herself for the accident, and takes an overdose. Max reaffirms his love for her, and together they scatter the ashes. Susannah decides she would like to start another family with Max, but discovers she can no longer have children. When they realise they will not be eligible to adopt they consider surrogacy, and approach Jacqui Dixon.

Lindsey sings Cher

8 Ron buys out Jacqui's partner in Bar Brookie. He moves into the bungalow and rents the house to the O'Leary family. Tinhead applies for the army but is rejected, failing the hearing test.

Jimmy and Jackie

Ollie in therapy

Bel and Danny Simpson

Shock for Max

9 The Simpsons go into therapy but Ollie finds the revelations about Georgia's pregnancy and termination too difficult to bear. Georgia gets a transfer at work, and she and Nat leave to live together. Ollie meets Eleanor Kitson in Bar Brookie, and Bel has a liaison with Mike Dixon. She and Ollie finally split up and Dan decides to live with Ollie. Eleanor moves in and confesses to Ollie that she has a long-lost daughter, Louise.

10 Mike publishes a book about his Bangkok experiences but he and Lindsey split up when he takes all the credit for her creative input. Jackie gives birth to William in June and Jimmy starts teacher training. Lindsey gets engaged to Peter but has an affair with Barry Grant.

Elaine and Gladys

David and Leanne

Tinhead's rejection

Barry and Lindsey

Callum Finnegan

DEATH

While 1996 in *Brookside* could be characterised by illicit affairs and drugs, 1997 was all about death – from the sudden and unexpected to the slow and lingering.

The car crash which saw the death of Max and Susannah Farnham's children, Matthew and Emily, would prove to be another memorable and moving *Brookside* story. Speaking to *The Liverpool Echo* in April that year, Karen Drury, who played Susannah Farnham, revealed: 'I had no idea what to expect filming the crash scenes. It really is the most horrendous accident and with so many people from the real-life emergency services around, it felt so realistic. At one point I was trapped in the car surrounded by paramedics and firemen trying to free me, and I know that everyone involved left the scene feeling that they would all drive very carefully in the future.'

In typical *Brookside* style, there were to be further twists on this horrific accident: Susannah had a glass of wine before getting into the car and although she was not over the limit there was the suggestion that this could have affected her judgement. Adding to her guilt was the fact that she had

At the wheel

The crash

Matthew is thrown from the car

Max and Susannah living in grief

Susannah's sister Lisa lends comfort

emerged from the accident relatively unscathed, although an infection which set in after her injuries would mean that she would no longer be able to have children, something she and Max longed for. *Brookside's* research had shown that adoption agencies would not consider the Farnhams whilst they were still grieving, and with Susannah unwilling to wait, surrogacy was the only solution. The surrogacy storyline involving Jacqui Dixon was now in place.

ISSUES IN BROOKSIDE: EUTHANASIA

Over five nights from June 30 to July 4, *Brookside* screened the assisted death of bone cancer sufferer Gladys Charlton. Channel Four's promotional trailers for this special five-nighter highlighted the key issues with a montage of words over action from the programme: 'PILLS... LOVE... LIVE', and, 'CONSEQUENCES'.

Over February and March that year, *Brookside* had held its usual storyline planning meetings in which the euthanasia storyline was discussed. From the start, it was felt that *Brookside* should not adopt a 'soap-box' approach. It was also acknowledged that it was important that the audience was aware of Gladys' desire to die. An early idea was for Mick and Elaine to find a stash of pills put aside by Gladys and confront her with them.

In May, Director Steve Garwood was considering the difficulties in shooting the death scenes: 'These are all interior scenes and a lot of them take place at night, which means that we'll have blacks [blinds] on the windows because we'll be shooting by day. And you can imagine what that will do when it's full of lights and people and it's June or May. It's going to be an incredibly hot, cramped and confined space... incredibly difficult working conditions, and to keep people's concentration up is going to be the hard thing. And God knows, it's going to be depressing.'

Later, however, Garwood would look back on the episode and note how successfully *Brookside* had married the intense scenes of Gladys' death with other lighter storylines: 'I take my hat off to these performers for getting the emotional intensity that they got – but also to those who were doing the other stuff, the light comedy scenes, who because of the pressures of the schedule very often had to play scenes which required just as much timing, just as much technical ability, but really fast. I think they did it convincingly, and I didn't have to worry so much about the way those scenes went together – I could take all that for granted.'

Independent journalist Suzanne Moore was complimentary of the finished episode: 'I think what was very important was the way Gladys' character was established as someone who was very sure what she wanted. She wanted to go on until she couldn't – which is actually quite life-enhancing.'

CHANNEL FIVE

On March 30, a fifth terrestrial channel began broadcasting. The channel's impact on *Brookside* would prove to be minimal, bar some speculation in the press that Phil Redmond might consider taking *Brookside* away from Channel Four. Apparently Channel Five wanted to 'buy-in' its success by acquiring ready-made talent and programmes.

'This is an issue I've been talking about for some time,' Redmond confirmed to *The Stage* in April, days after the launch. 'In a few years it won't be channels people have a loyalty to, but programmes, and this will drive up the cost of talent. But whatever the situation, we won't be making any moves for a while.'

Redmond never felt compelled to up-sticks and take *Brookside* elsewhere, having a loyalty to the programme's original channel.

REACTION

In response to *Brookside's* five-nighter storyline on euthanasia, Channel Four's *Right to Reply* programme broadcast a special edition in which health carers discussed the episodes. They attacked *Brookside* for its 'melodramatic situation' and accused it of scare-mongering, something that irritated *Brookside's* Producers as they had been careful to get specialist medical advice on the issue. As if to support the producers' case, a Teletext poll showed that four out of five viewers backed the programme's handling of this difficult subject.

MERCHANDISE

Following the template established in 1995 with *Brookside: The Women*, the video release of *Brookside: The Men* (Channel Four Video) proved to be another success this year. For this edition Vince Earl (Ron Dixon), Steven Pinder (Max Farnham), Dean Sullivan (Jimmy Corkhill), John McArdle (Billy Corkhill), Brian Regan (Terry Sullivan) and Michael Starke (Sinbad) gathered together in the back garden of No. 7 Brookside Close to talk about their most memorable moments in the programme. As ever, Phil Redmond chaired the discussion.

Alongside this, 1997 was also notable for the release of *Brookside: The Backstage Tour* (Channel Four Video). Originally set to be hosted by Michael Starke (Sinbad), Dean Sullivan (Jimmy Corkhill), John Burgess (David Crosbie) and Sarah White (Bev McLoughlin), the final release actually paired the latter two with Alexandra Fletcher (Jacqui Dixon) and Diane Burke (Katie Rogers). The actors hosted an 'access-all-areas' tour of *Brookside*, mixed in with archive footage. This video could also boast something of an exclusive: a look at the alternative ending filmed for the Jordache trial in 1995 which depicted events taking a much happier turn for Beth and Mandy.

The Lost Weekend (Polygram Filmed Entertainment), also released this year, marked another evolution in *Brookside's* video library, featuring a specially shot story that occurred 'in-between' events depicted during the programme's regular on-screen episodes. 'Barry Grant's back with a vengeance' ran the promotional text, 'and reunited with his mother Sheila as sinister events conspire to bring the Corkhills and the Grants together again.' *Brookside's* viewers would hear reference to the weekend, while the video revealed what actually happened. *The Lost Weekend* was also notable in that it was classified as an '18' certificate, treating issues in a manner that would have been difficult for *Brookside* to do in its regular slot on Channel Four.

Lindsey Corkhill

BROOKSIDE: Episodes 1993–2157
WRITERS: Joe Ainsworth, Maurice Bessman,
Roy Boulter, Peter Cox, Shaun Duggan, Julie Jones, Sue Mooney,
Barbara Phillips, Nick Saltrese, Chris Webb, Barry Woodward

DIRECTORS: Chris Bernard, Darrol Blake, Mervin Cumming, Jude Dine,
Steve Finn, Keith Gabriel, Nicky Higgens, Maurice Hutchinson,
Chris Johnson, Dominic Keavey, Michael Kerrigan,
Brian Morgan, Peter Rose, Michael Samuels, Pip Short,
Rupert Such, Jeremy Summers, Bob Thomson, Patrick Tucker

TRANSMISSION: January 2–December 30

1998

HOUSE BY HOUSE

5 Mick is acquitted of Gladys' murder. He decides that Brookside Comprehensive is failing Leo, and that Gemma will go to private school.

6 David goes out with Ron's ex, Molly Marchbank, and moves to her country estate, Bressingham Hall. Ron moves into the Parade flats where there is an explosion, and the Shadwicks arrive. Jason's girlfriend Katrina tells him she is pregnant and they opt to have a termination. Nikki is raped at a Christmas party when her drink is spiked.

7 Jacqui is pregnant with Max's baby. Max and Susannah get married, and Susannah discovers she too is now pregnant. Jacqui gives birth to Harry in September. Susannah finds out about Max's affair with Faye, which has been going on for 20 years and throws him out. At Christmas, she and Greg Shadwick share a kiss.

Susannah and Max

Gas cooker for Ron

Molly's grand home

Off comes Lindsey's ring

Susannah and Max Farnham re-marry

End for Jimmy?

8 Sinbad moves in with Carmel, however she is unable to forgive his part in the explosion when Ben finds out his paralysis is permanent. Tinhead swears revenge. Carmel leaves the Close to be near Ben who is moved to a rehabilitation unit. Tinhead tries to run Sinbad over but drives into a lake, leaving Sinbad to save his life. Tinhead moves in with Mick and Leo as the Musgroves arrive.

9 Louise tracks down her father, an animal rights activist Marcus Seddon, who is serving a prison sentence. They spend time together when he is released. Eleanor and Marcus become closer and eventually make love in her office, but she decides to stick with Ollie and they agree to marry. Marcus takes them all hostage on holiday, resulting in a cliff-side tussle that brings about his death. The coroner's verdict is accidental death. Ollie is unable to forgive Eleanor, and he and Danny leave.

Close explodes

10 Gary turns up, and when Lindsey asks for a divorce he demands money and access visits to Kylie. He starts legal proceedings and harasses Lindsey, who, in desperation, threatens him with a gun. Gary backs down and Lindsey gets her divorce. Lindsey and Peter get married. Using forged certificates Jimmy gets onto a teacher training course which he passes, leading to a job at Brookside Comprehensive.

Megan Brindley and Mike Dixon

THE PARADE

Ron buys a second-hand cooker from Sinbad and connects it himself, causing a major explosion. Ron finds out he has a daughter, Megan, from his affair with Anthea Brindley 20 years ago. Anthea proposes to Ron. Ron sees Bev shoplifting and persuades Mike to take her in, for Josh's sake. Jacqui has a launch party for The Millennium Club.

'RE-TUNING THE PROGRAMME'

1998 brought the publication of the *Brookside* book, *Total Brookside*. As ever, Phil Redmond's contribution signalled the way ahead for his programme and he talked about the new family created to live on the Close, the Shadwicks. 'Over the past few months,' he wrote, 'we've... been re-tuning the programme, introducing new characters like the Shadwicks who represent the shift in emphasis. Greg Shadwick served his time on the maintenance gangs at Cammell-Laird, but now he is self-employed and wants to control his own destiny. And his wife Margi is a trade union representative in the food processing industry so we have characters who will take part in some of the debates which are currently affecting the country, such as what are New Labour going to do about health, welfare and education? And where is the money going to come from for welfare to work?'

Redmond was in the mood to be reflective, feeling that the *Brookside* of 1998 was closer to the programme that launched in 1982 than it had been during the nineties: 'When we started out, we had the Collins, the Grants, the Huntingtons and the Taylors as the four elements of society on the Close. The Collins represented the management capitalist leg; the Grants represented the trade union movement; the Huntingtons were a young professional couple; and the Taylors represented the black economy... Now we've got the same range. The Farnhams represent the enterprise culture; the Shadwicks represent the unions; Ollie and Eleanor are the professionals; and Jimmy's still being a scally with his forged teaching certificates.'

THE UNLUCKIEST HOUSE IN THE WORLD?

With another five-nighter on the way, *Brookside* was able to promote the event when Channel Four decided to theme a night around Merseyside the weekend before the first episode went out. Naturally asked to contribute to the evening's entertainment, Mersey Television's Conker Boy Films produced the documentary *No.10: The Unluckiest House in the World?*, a documentary about the second most famous No.10 in Britain. A nostalgic treat, it also served successfully to warm up the audience for a special week on *Brookside...*

Nikki, Emily, Margi, Greg and Jason Shadwick

THE EXPLOSION

'It's your decision, it's either your legs or the girl drowns.'

The explosion on Brookside Parade was described by Phil Redmond at the time as 'one of the most spectacular events in the programme's history'.

The planned storyline had Ron Dixon trying to install a gas cooker he had bought from Sinbad, only to bring about a massive gas explosion that would devastate much of the Parade. To achieve this on screen was a massive undertaking.

Christmas Day at the Dixons

Nikki Shadwick and Luke Musgrove

Ron's flat explodes

Emily Shadwick

The events of Friday the 13th

The Director for the episode, Steve Finn, termed it a 'nightmare' to organise, confirming to *The Liverpool Echo* that 'it's the biggest thing we've ever done and there is so much to think about. There are major safety considerations.'

Meanwhile, the design department had to depict the damage wrought. Yam Rowlands, Mersey Television's current Head of Design recalls: 'This was the biggest challenge our department had faced on *Brookside*, not only from a special effects point of view, but in duplicating a number of sets so that we could shoot through the floor between Ron's flat and Sinbad's shop.'

Meanwhile, the production team on *Brookside* had to make sure that all aspects of the spectacular event were properly researched so as to be as realistic as possible. So in addition to exploring the effects of the explosion with the emergency services, they also spoke to utilities companies (for example, to find out how a gas explosion is dealt with), investigated paediatric neurosurgery (for Kylie's head injury), researched how a medical aid team operates (when Sinbad nearly lost his legs so that the team could rescue Kylie from

Lindsey and Peter Phelan

water below) and looked into spinal injury (for Ben the fireman's injured back).

The story did not end there, however, with repercussions continuing for Ron and Sinbad when the Health and Safety Executives got involved. There would be all sorts of ripples felt for months.

Jimmy Corkhill in class

MERCHANDISE

Friday the 13th (Polygram Filmed Entertainment) was *Brookside's* video release for this year and something of a sequel to *The Lost Weekend*. Common to both was the return of Sue Johnston to the role of Sheila Grant, who revealed that she had separated from Billy Corkhill some time after leaving the Close.

As part of an evening of programmes themed around Merseyside that year, Channel Four's Stuart Cosgrove commissioned a documentary from *Brookside* about its most infamous property – *No.10: The Unluckiest House in the World?* The programme reunited several actors whose characters had lived in No.10 Brookside Close. Alongside this, the documentary invited famous *Brookside* fans to share their favourite memories of the house. Shortly afterwards, a spin-off 'talking book' was released, read by Michael Starke (Sinbad), detailing the

house's unique history.

1998 also saw the publication of another Geoff Tibball's *Brookside* book, *Total Brookside* (Ebury Press). With a month-by-month history of events on the Close and a reproduction of the script for episode one, alongside miscellaneous interviews and character profiles, *Total Brookside* is a *Brookside* fan's bible.

Rachel Jordache and Mike Dixon

David 'Bing' Crosbie and Molly Marchbank

Eleanor Kitson

Jacqui, Susannah and Lindsey

REACTION

Writing in the *Radio Times* in May, columnist Alison Graham reflected on the five-nighter: 'Brookside loves a good disaster. Someone on the production team must take a perverse pleasure in watching blue flashing lights and fire engines.'

Seeds being sown for what would become 'Brookie Basics' in 1999 caught the attention of the *Mirror* in September: 'Education Secretary David Blunkett has signed up top soaps... *Brookside* and children's drama *Grange Hill* in the fight to beat illiteracy. Key storylines are to show how reading difficulties can be overcome. *The Guardian* also noted: 'Former "bad boy" Jimmy Corkhill's new career as a teacher at Brookside Comprehensive is already helping to focus on classroom activities and topical education themes.'

Meanwhile the second five-nighter in November was keenly observed by the *TV Times* which commented: 'Marrying a Corkhill was never going to be easy but Peter finds it almost impossible in the five-night special this week. Luckily for Sam Kane [who plays Peter], the filming proved to be fun... thanks to the appearance of his real life wife, Linda Lusardi!' At the same time, *Friday the 13th* was also released, prompting *Inside Soap* to declare 'this video is every bit as compelling as last year's offering', whilst *Woman* magazine concluded that *Friday the 13th* was 'not to be missed by any true soap addict'.

Susannah Farnham with Emma and Harry

BROOKSIDE: Episodes 2158–2316
WRITERS: Maurice Bessman, Roy Boulter, Gary Brown, Richard Burke,
Peter Cox, Bill Dawson, Shaun Duggan, John Fay, Julie Jones, Sue Mooney,
Carmel Morgan, Debbie Oates, Barbara Phillips, Jane Pritchard,
Chris Webb, Barry Woodward, David Young

DIRECTORS: Chris Bernard, Darrol Blake, Mervin Cumming, Jude Dine,
Haldane Duncan, Steve Finn, Keith Gabriel, Tony Garner, Nicky Higgens,
Maurice Hutchinson, Michael Kerrigan, Peter Rose, Pip Short,
Jeremy Summers, Garth Tucker, Patrick Tucker, Roger Tucker

TRANSMISSION: January 1 – December 31

1999

HOUSE BY HOUSE

5 Yvonne Johnson asks Mick to let Jerome move in and Sinbad is devastated to find out that Mandy is getting remarried. Mick and Sinbad are assaulted by Josh and his racist gang, and Sinbad suffers permanent damage to his hearing. Violence escalates, ending only when Josh horrifically sets fire to himself with a petrol bomb meant for Mick. Gemma is hospitalised after taking Ecstasy.

6 Greg and Susannah's affair continues but Jessie catches them. Greg decides to leave Margi for Susannah but is killed when the Millennium Club blows up. Jason also dies in the carnage. Margi moves to Brussels, and Nikki turns to drink. Emily and Tim start going out, while Nikki is kidnapped by a fellow student, Harvey. She escapes and he is arrested. Jessie moves in to look after the girls. Luke Musgrove admits to Nikki that he did rape her.

7 Susannah gives birth to Emma with Greg by her side. She is hurt in the Millennium Club blast, and lies seriously ill in hospital. Max arrives back on the Close to take care of the children. When Margi tries to strangle Susannah, Max moves in to protect her.

Mick injured

Sinbad hurt

Luke Musgrove

Gemma takes ecstacy

Susannah and Greg in Millennium Club blast rubble

131

Millennium Club explosion

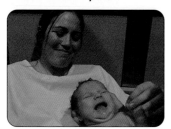

Rachel and Beth

8 Luke Musgrove is charged with Nikki's rape but he is acquitted. Niamh's illiteracy is revealed and she plucks up the courage to attend an adult literacy centre. The family is devastated by Luke's Christmas confession that he raped Nikki. Joey leaves when Niamh refuses to send Luke back to Ireland.

9 Peter has an affair and dumps Lindsey. Lindsey steals £60,000 and a car from Callum Finnegan, and uses it to buy Barry out of the Millennium Club. Rose Finnegan demands the money back from Lindsey by the end of the year. Lindsey hires a hitman to sort out Callum, but Callum kills him first and has Lindsey beaten up. When she is unable to pay up by the year's end, Rose installs drug dealers in the club.

10 Jimmy and Jackie's relationship goes through a difficult time. Jimmy tells her that he forged his certificates to become a teacher. Jackie, suspecting he is having an affair with a colleague, blows his secret and Jimmy is sacked. His behaviour becomes increasingly eccentric.

THE PARADE

Ron and Anthea get engaged and are married later in the year. Ron opens his new business, Great Grannies. Anthea's smear test shows pre-cancerous cells. Ron stores bleach in lemonade bottles which baby Ruth drinks, prompting Sinbad to attack Ron. Rachel overcomes her fears about relationships and finally commits to Mike. She discovers she is pregnant and they get engaged in December. She gives birth to Beth at Christmas. Victoria Seagram, Nathan Cuddington and Dr Darren Roebuck move into one of the flats and when Darren declares his love for Victoria, they start a relationship. Her estranged husband Mark tells them he has Motor Neurone Disease, and Victoria sacrifices her relationship with Darren out of pity. Mark falls down the stairs and dies – but was it a suicide bid? Jacqui dates Nathan and discovers he has a country seat – Cuddington Hall. Nathan proposes to Jacqui in December.

REDEEMING JIMMY

The nineties had been difficult for Jimmy Corkhill. He had started the decade in conflict with gangster Jimmy Godden and ended it being dismissed from his job as a schoolteacher. In the intervening years he had become reconciled – separated – and reconciled again with his wife; turned to drugs and in doing so brought about the death of Tony Dixon, Frank Rogers and (indirectly) Shane Cochran; served a prison sentence; experienced the death of one son and the birth of another, and started the slow slide into bi-polar disorder (manic depression).

No one could seriously claim that Jimmy has not lived through some strange times, however long-term *Brookside* writer Barry Woodward believes that 'he's one of our most interesting characters and he's massively popular with our viewers. To me his life seems entirely plausible. There's always been that crazy edge to everything he's done, especially when he was into drugs and petty crime scams.'

As for Jimmy becoming a schoolteacher, this was part of a plan to 'redeem' the character following his drug-fuelled years and the deaths that accrued as a result. He was to become part of the normal working population, but with his own skew-way of looking at things.

Throughout 1999, it would become more obvious that Jimmy was having mental health problems. By the end of the year he would no longer be teaching. But his battle with bi-polar disorder would not end there.

Jimmy sees the headmaster

Matt Musgrove and the disciples of Shad

AFTERMATH

In much the same way that *Brookside* was following-up Jimmy's storyline as set in motion the previous year, in 1999, the programme would also pick up on the aftermath of Nikki Shadwick's drug rape the previous Christmas.

In basing a story around drug rape, *Brookside* was again proving itself to be topical in its choice of storylines. Certainly it was one of the first drama serials on television to tackle a subject which in the late nineties was still relatively unheard of. Indeed, the first drug rape charity did not come into being until

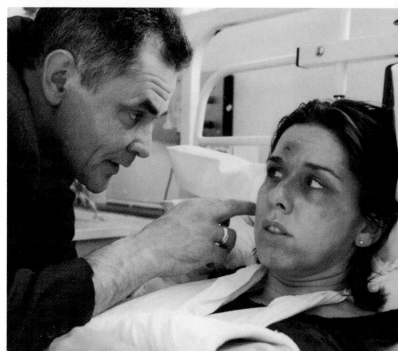

Top right to bottom right: Callum Finnegan turns the tables on Lindsey Corkhill

1999. In preparing for the storyline, *Brookside* benefited from the assistance of local rape and sexual assault charities, as well as police Family Support Units. The programme's sensitive handling of the issue was roundly praised.

Looking at the aftermath of the rape, *Brookside* depicted Nikki's subsequent alcohol abuse, turning to the Merseyside and Cheshire Alcohol Service and also Alcohol Concern.

Top: Nikki and Harvey; Above: Luke Musgrove on trial

Luke Musgrove was eventually accused of drug-raping Nikki, however when it went to court he was controversially found not guilty. As with the Jordache trial of 1995, here was another example of *Brookside* pursuing realism rather than popular feeling. In addition to providing a memorable verdict, the trial also carved out a special place in *Brookside* history with the debut of a new title sequence on its first day, on June 29.

Greg and Susannah's illicit affair

CHANGING THE TITLE SEQUENCE

Original titles

After the explosion last year, Brookside Parade had been rebuilt. This prompted the decision to update *Brookside's* titles, incorporating the new-look Parade. Lee Hardman, Producer in Mersey Television's Conker Media (a division responsible for the company's websites, factual and features programming), was given the

New titles

job of making the changes. In discussion with Phil Redmond, the decision was taken to bring about a level of synergy between *Brookside's* on-screen visuals and those of its official website, *www.brookside.com*, which had been launched the previous year.

Completed in a relatively short space of time, the new titles included footage from the preceding version, but also a new sequence following a young girl as she cycled from the Parade to the Close.

Hardman remembers that the new title sequence was well received, with the Super-8 shots approaching each of the doors in turn coming in for particular praise from Channel Four, who felt this was an effective way to segue into the programme. The idea of incorporating a trailer for the next episode in the closing credits sequence was also welcomed and it is an innovation that has been much imitated since.

Max and Niamh get close

Top: Mick sees racist graffiti; Middle: Shelley and Jackie Corkhill;
Bottom: Shelley and Lindsey Corkhill

135

BROOKIE BASICS

Brookside has displayed an enduring concern for literacy problems since its earliest days. In 1998, Phil Redmond had been approached to contribute to the government's National Year of Reading and so decided to include a storyline detailing Niamh Musgrove's illiteracy into *Brookside* for 1999.

This led to the launch in February of the 'Brookie Basics' adult literacy project in association with Channel Four, Broadcasting Support Services, The Department for Education and Employment, Learning Direct and Liverpool Community College who developed teaching aid materials that were used in the scheme. The creation of 'Brookie Basic' centres nationwide followed on, and courses aimed at adults who wanted to improve their literacy skills.

Niamh's storyline began at the end of April and was accompanied by a help line number for people to call. It prompted thousands of telephone calls to 'Brookie Basic' centres who were then in a position to assist, thanks to a wide range of *Brookside* themed learning materials – one being a special 'Brookie Basics' branded edition of Collins' English Dictionary. A supplementary video, *What's In It For Me?* was also released to great critical acclaim.

Meanwhile, Rt Hon David Blunkett MP, Secretary of State for Education and Employment spoke about why the government had asked *Brookside* to assist: *Brookside's* made a big difference because it was the first programme to highlight just how critical the literacy programme was. We've gained enormously from others being prepared to join in once they saw that there was a commitment from Phil Redmond and from those putting *Brookside* together, and it's important because it gets a very critical message across to those who would otherwise be turned off from learning.'

Following up on the good work done by 'Brookie Basics', the Production Company, Planet Wild, put together three five-minute documentaries following the fortunes of just a handful of participants on the course. They were shown preceding regular episodes of *Brookside* later in the year.

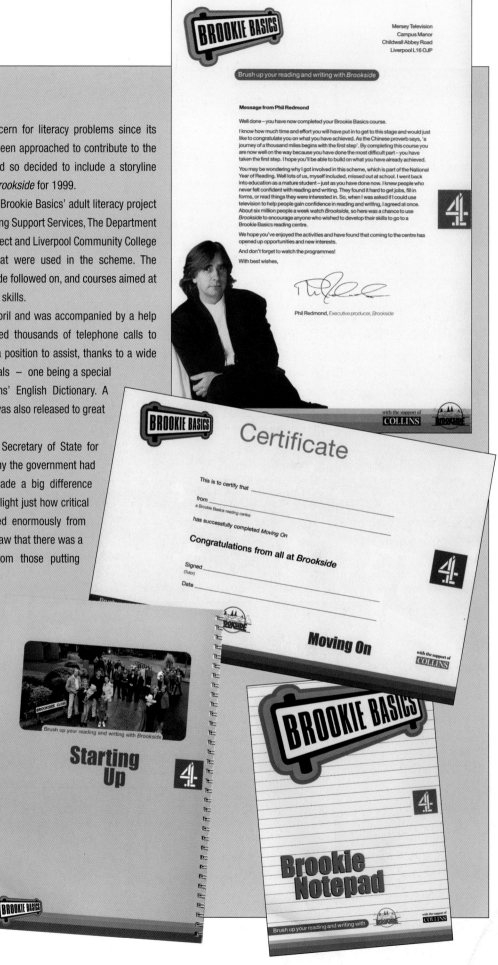

MERCHANDISE

Alongside the material released to support the 'Brookie Basics' campaign (which ranged from posters to workbooks), 1999 saw *Brookside's* final video release to date: *Brookside: Double Take* (Universal Pictures Video). With the working-title *Altered Egos*, here was yet another reinvention of the format, presenting a spoof behind-the-scenes documentary, also featuring cameos from members of the cast of *Hollyoaks*.

Right: Lindsey catches Peter with Frankie

REACTION

In August, *The Guardian* met with Phil Redmond and new Series Producer Paul Marquess. It quoted Redmond as saying *Brookside* was taking a 'back to basics' approach and that from now on, 'more action will take place in the olde worlde Close, less in the newfangled Parade.'

Marquess, meanwhile, told the paper: 'One of the strengths we can exploit is social realism, the fact that in *Brookside* you can actually look out of the windows of the houses. The other soaps are better resourced, but their grammar is still very theatrical; you can't follow someone into or out of the café in *EastEnders*, for example. *Brookside* has much more the feel of a docu-soap, and I want to continue loosening up the camera style.'

Elsewhere, Suzanne Collins, who played Nikki Shadwick, found herself becoming something of an icon for victims of drug rape. As a result she received hundreds of letters from women across the country who identified with her character and had similarly had to battle to overcome this problem.

The 'Brookie Basics' campaign was also eliciting a huge response, typical of the hundreds received is the report of 27-year-old Joanne Kettles in Cornwall who benefited from the campaign. She revealed: 'At school, I had some negative experiences and I didn't want to learn but this has been so different. Because I like *Brookside* and was interested in the characters, I could associate with learning more.'

Nathan Cuddington, Jacqui Dixon, Rachel Jordache and Mike Dixon

Prime suspects – Emily, Mick, Max and Jacqui

BROOKSIDE: Episodes 2317–2479

WRITERS: Maurice Bessman, Roy Boulter, Richard Burke, Marianne Colbran, Peter Cox, Arthur Ellison, John Fay, Jo Fraser, Ed Jones, Sue Mooney, Carmel Morgan, Debbie Oates, Gareth Roberts, Heather Robson, Trea Smallcombe, Barry Woodward, David Young

DIRECTORS: Adrian Bean, Darrol Blake, Sylvie Boden, Emma Bodger, Nigel Bristow, Mervin Cumming, Robert Delamere, Haldane Duncan, Steve Finn, Tony Garner, Tim Holloway, Julian Holmes, Maurice Hutchinson, Nigel Keen, Daniella Newman, Nic Phillips, Pip Short, Jeremy Summers, Garth Tucker, Patrick Tucker, Jeremy Webb

TRANSMISSION: January 4 – December 29

2000

HOUSE BY HOUSE

5 Gemma leaves the Close to go to live with Josie. Sinbad starts voluntary work at a school for the deaf but is accused of sexual abuse. He is arrested and is devastated to find out how few people trust him. He is cleared but, disappointed and disillusioned, he leaves the Close. Leo is accepted by the police force.

Shock for Sinbad

6 Ray moves in with Jessie, and at Christmas she agrees to marry him. Tim and Emily plan revenge on Susannah and gradually descend into a life of crime, with Tim ending up in prison.

7 Susannah starts affairs with Mick and Darren. Mick asks Susannah to marry him and she accepts, but continues seeing Darren. As Mick and Darren find out about each other, Max argues with Susannah, and in a tussle he pushes her down the stairs to her death. The police conclude it was accidental death and Max moves in. He contemplates suicide but is thwarted by the arrival of Jacqui.

Emily and Tim

Max sees Mick with Susannah

139

The Murrays arrive

8 Niamh moves the whole family to Ireland and Sinbad lets the house to Mike, Rachel and Katie. Ron leaves Anthea and moves in too. Nathan sacks Katie after a breach of confidence which leads to Katie and Jacqui falling out. Jacqui and Rachel have a hen party in Benidorm where Jacqui meets Robbie Moffat. Rachel and Mike get married at Cuddington Hall, but Nathan stops his ceremony as he doesn't think Jacqui loves him. Robbie arrives in the Parade and Jacqui starts dating him, whilst Katie sees his brother Clint. Mike is in a car crash at Christmas – and is paralysed as a result.

9 The Murrays arrive. Diane and Marty are trying for a baby, and start fertility treatment. In November she has a positive pregnancy test but worries she is losing the baby at Christmas.

10 Jimmy breaks down completely and Jackie agrees to have him sectioned. Shelley breaks with Lindsey, and pursues Jackie. Jackie is terrified that Shelley will tell Lindsey about the night they spent together. Lindsey is shocked when she finds out.

Jimmy leaves home

THE PARADE

Bev buys the bar and renames it Bev's Bar. Darren comforts Victoria who feels guilty about Mark's death. He asks her to marry him. Victoria reveals she is pregnant and has an abortion, despite Darren's feelings. She is shocked by his affair with Susannah.

RETURNS, REINVENTIONS AND INTRODUCTIONS

In 2000, *Brookside* would welcome a number of returning characters: Leanne Powell (last seen in 1997), Nisha Batra (1990), Bev McLoughlin (1996) and Josie Johnson (1993) all showed up unexpectedly. Whilst Josie was only visiting, Leanne, Nisha and Bev were here to stay.

In the case of Vicky Gates (Leanne), Producer Paul Marquess had previously worked with her on the Sky One/Channel Four soap *Springhill* and had been extremely impressed with her performance. Her character had last been seen in *Brookside* being sentenced to prison for throwing corrosive liquid in Jacqui Dixon's eyes. Sunetra Sarker had also appeared in *Brookside* before as Nisha, Sammy Rogers' friend who had been caught up in the car crash in 1990. Additionally, Bev, with her 'complex' relationship with the Dixons, was also to return to the Close. All characters proved as successful (if not more so) second time around.

Marquess also heralded the introduction of a new family to the Close: 'The Murrays are an ordinary working-class Liverpool family,' he explained, 'who will play a key role in taking *Brookside* back to basics.' They would reach our screens on March 28.

Finally, an existing character, Emily Shadwick, was reinvented. Previously she had been a normal school girl, now she was transformed into a glamorous rebel wildchild.

Emily and Tim get close

Susannah's demise

SINBAD'S DEPARTURE

This year would also see a long-term *Brookside* character leave. Sinbad would be falsely accused of sexually abusing a child. Typically for *Brookside* it was to be another controversial storyline, revolving around misconception rather than actual sexual abuse and showing the damage false accusations can do. Although vindicated by the end of the story, Sinbad was left a broken man who had discovered that the trust he had enjoyed with his friends was not as strong as he had thought.

PRODUCING BROOKSIDE: PAUL MARQUESS

Born in Belfast, Paul Marquess studied drama at Manchester University and joined Granada Television in 1993 where he worked as a Story Editor on *Coronation Street* and as a consultant and writer on *Family Affairs*. Marquess also produced the soap *Springhill* for Sky One and the *Coronation Street* video, *Coronation Street: Viva Las Vegas!* before moving onto the drama, *Picking Up The Pieces*. He joined *Brookside* as Series Producer in 1999, stating that he had watched the programme since its first episode and liked its political edge.

Marquess left *Brookside* in 2001 to become Executive Producer on *The Bill*.

'It's a very sensitive storyline,' Paul Marquess told *The Times*, 'but I'm planning it very deliberately not to be a mystery over whether he did it or not. If I wanted to do it just for ratings then I would have made it a "did he, didn't he" affair. But I think that would have been grubby.'

Michael Starke, who played Sinbad, did have some concerns, however. 'I have mixed feelings,' he said. 'On the one hand it is challenging and as an actor you do want challenges, but on the other you weigh up the implications. But any good story has a degree of discomfort and it is good that we are tackling the subject in such a responsible way.'

In all, it made a memorable and challenging exit for one of *Brookside's* most likeable characters, although as Starke noted, 'at the end of the day we leave the door open.'

REACTION

Vicky Spavin in *The Daily Record* was looking forward to Jacqui's hen party in Benidorm. 'It wasn't all sangria and paella for the six actresses during filming,' she wrote. 'Firstly they were afraid of looking awful in their bikinis – although they needn't have worried. And then they had some poor weather to contend with. The two-week shoot was done in March, and the stars had to turn out in their skimpy clothes even when the weather was chilly. Whatever the weather back at the Close, things won't be dull when the holiday hi-jinks are revealed.'

Emily and Tim get married

BROOKSIDE: Episodes 2480–2640
WRITERS: Maurice Bessman, Roy Boulter, Marianne Colbran,
Peter Cox, Arthur Ellison, John Fay, Tom Higgins, Ed Jones,
Jan McVerry, Sue Mooney, Carmel Morgan, Debbie Oates, Gareth Roberts,
Heather Robson, Trea Smallcombe, Barry Woodward, David Young

DIRECTORS: Adrian Bean, Darrol Blake, Emma Bodger, Viv Cozens,
Mervin Cumming, Robert Delamere, Steve Finn, Tony Garner, Maurice Hutchinson,
Nigel Keen, Daikin Marsh, Paul Murphy, Daniella Newman,
Nic Phillips, Jeremy Summers, Patrick Tucker, Ali Turnbull, David Winn

TRANSMISSION: January 2 – December 26

2001

HOUSE BY HOUSE

5 Jerome has an affair with Nisha Batra. Mick and Yvonne decide to try to make a go of it, and Yvonne moves in. Leo sleeps with Adele Murray and gets her pregnant. Mick makes him leave Liverpool. Mick proposes to Yvonne but she leaves him, taking Jerome with her. Emily and Tim move into No.10 and Mick is left alone. Jimmy manages to talk around a suicidal Mick who then decides to leave the Close for a fresh start.

6 Ray and Jessie get married. Emily goes topless for some glamour shots and Tim is shocked and teased when he sees them in a magazine in prison. Jessie buys the bungalow. Tim and Emily are reunited when he gets out of prison and they marry. Nikki proposes to Jerome and he accepts. At their engagement party Nikki cracks – she's known about his affair all along. The relationship is over.

7 Jacqui tries to help Max get over Susannah's death. He allows her more input into Harry's upbringing and they start a relationship. Jacqui moves in with Max but Robbie kidnaps baby Harry. Harry is recovered safely but there is no evidence to link Robbie to the crime. Max confesses to Jacqui about Susannah's death but the couple still marry.

Jacqui and Max marry

Adele Murray

Anthea Dixon

Robbie Moffat

Ron in the dock

Emily O'Leary

8 Mike is told he will be confined to a wheelchair as his and Rachel's financial problems get worse. Ron, Anthea, Jessie, Ray and his mother Kitty are bound and gagged when the Dixons' is raided at Robbie's behest. Robbie burgles the Dixon household again and Ron is furious. Tim gets Ron a gun and when Robbie returns to the house again, Ron shoots Clint who had only gone in to get Robbie out. With Anthea uncertain whether she can lie for Ron in court about the shooting, their marriage breaks-up and she leaves. Ron's found not guilty of murder and manslaughter, but receives a nine month prison sentence for pleading guilty to the possession of a firearm.

Jimmy's decline

9 Diane loses the baby. Marty borrows money to pay for IVF, but the treatment is unsuccessful. Anthony is being bullied at school by two girls, Imelda and Paige. Adele discovers she is pregnant by Leo and despite pressure from Diane, she goes through with an abortion.

10 After Jackie tells Jimmy about Shelley, he moves into the extension and starts divorce proceedings. Despite a brief reconciliation, Jackie and Jimmy separate. Tim and Emily move in. Jimmy holds a family reunion for his 50th but only Rod comes. Lindsey leaves for a job in Newcastle. At Christmas, a failed lorry-jacking job sees Tim almost drowning in the Mersey.

Susannah's funeral

THE PARADE

Bev marries Lance's Brazilian boyfriend, Fred, so he can stay in the country. Katie and Clint plan to leave for Spain but after he is killed by Ron, Katie falls into a depression. Darren and Victoria make a spur-of-the-moment decision and leave. Convinced by Leanne that the authorities are after her, Bev goes on the run leaving Leanne in charge of the bar. Sammy Rogers returns and tries to set a honey trap for Max.

Christie at the wheel

CHANGING RELATIONSHIPS

2001 was to be another notable year of change in *Brookside*. The death of Susannah Farnham in November 2000, with its 'Whodunit?' plot and memorable revelation of who was responsible had opened up the possibility of a romance between Max Farnham and Jacqui Dixon. Equally dramatic events this year, however, would bring about the end of Ron and Anthea Dixon's marriage, whilst Adele Murray would suffer from taking her relationship with Leo Johnson a step too far.

THE DEATH OF CLINT MOFFAT

It was to be Ron's storyline that would dominate 2001. Having been victimised by Robbie Moffat he had acquired a shotgun in the belief that it would enable him to protect his family. In a traditional *Brookside* twist of fate, Ron had ended up shooting Robbie's brother – Clint – whom he had mistakenly thought was trying to burgle his house. But was *Brookside* drawing on the real-life case of Tony Martin, the Norfolk farmer who had been imprisoned for shooting an intruder into his home? David Hanson, then a Producer on

Brookside, before becoming Senior Producer at the end of that year, remembers how the story came about: 'There was a lot of debate at the time about what rights homeowners have to defend their property. We felt that Ron was the ideal character to explore this with, but the storyline was planned before the Tony Martin case. What interested us the most, however, was the effect that Ron's actions would have on him, his wife, his family – and others affected by them. This is part of the joy of working in a creative industry – with the Ron/Clint storyline we were able to take one of *Brookside's* most long-lasting friendships – that between Jacqui and Katie – and send it in a totally new direction.'

The storyline that unfolded was a gripping and convincing study of the difficult issue of 'justifiable force', as well as detailing the fallout of a violent death and its effect

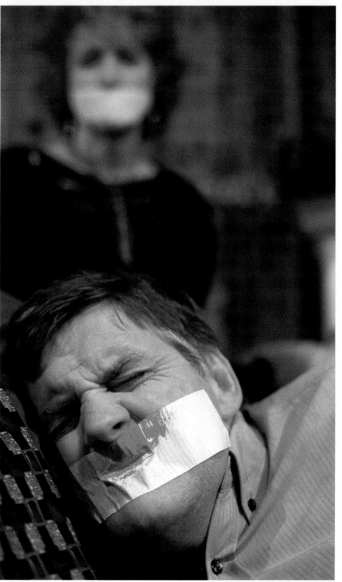

PLAYING THE DIXONS

Vince Earl (Ron Dixon)

Born in 1944 in Birkenhead, Vince Earl's roots lie in Variety. In the 1960s, he enjoyed a successful career as a pop singer and once shared the same stage as *The Beatles*. His credits include Alan Bleasdale's *Boys From the Black Stuff* and the film *No Surrender*, as well as a regular slot on Granada's 1970's stand-up series, *The Comedians*. An accomplished after-dinner speaker, Earl was working on a cruise ship when he was asked to read for the part of Ron Dixon and joined *Brookside* in 1990.

Paul Byatt (Mike Dixon)

Born in December 1971, Byatt was a member of a youth theatre whilst still at school but did not have any plans to get into acting full time. Byatt was due to attend university to take up a sound engineering course when he auditioned for *Brookside*. Still with the programme, he has said that he liked the edge to his character when he was younger, but is enjoying playing Mike Dixon as a father figure.

Alexandra Fletcher (Jacqui Farnham, née Dixon)

Born in 1976, Alexandra Fletcher first appeared on television in the children's series *Why Don't You?* at the age of 11. She won the role of Jacqui in 1990. Fletcher has described her character as 'uptight and spitfire-like' although feels that recently, Jacqui has become much warmer. Her on-screen marriage to Max Farnham in 2001 has provided Fletcher with new facets to explore in the role.

Above: Ron gets a gun from Tim

Left: Anthea and Ron, gagged by intruders

145

Jacqui, Anthea and Mike wonder if Ron will be found guilty

on all those connected to it – the perpetrator has to face the consequences of trial and imprisonment, his family have to decide whether to support him, whilst the victim's loved-ones fall into grief and resentment.

The resulting court case provided another legal set-piece to stand alongside any in *Brookside's* history.

ADELE'S PREGNANCY

Elsewhere, *Brookside* returned to a theme it had tackled before in its 19-year history – teenage pregnancy. Adele Murray, however, characterised as 'sensible'

Robbie seeks revenge on Ron

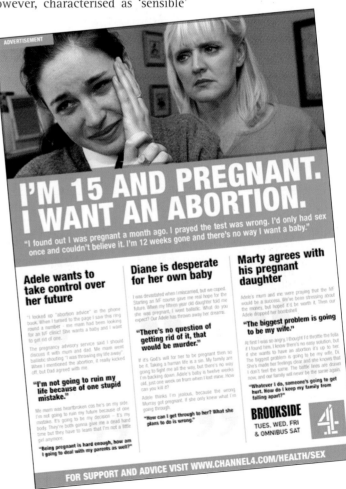

Promoting the story

Adele longs for Leo Johnson

Jerome and Nisha behind Nikki

Nikki spies Jerome and Nisha

Right: Nikki and Jerome

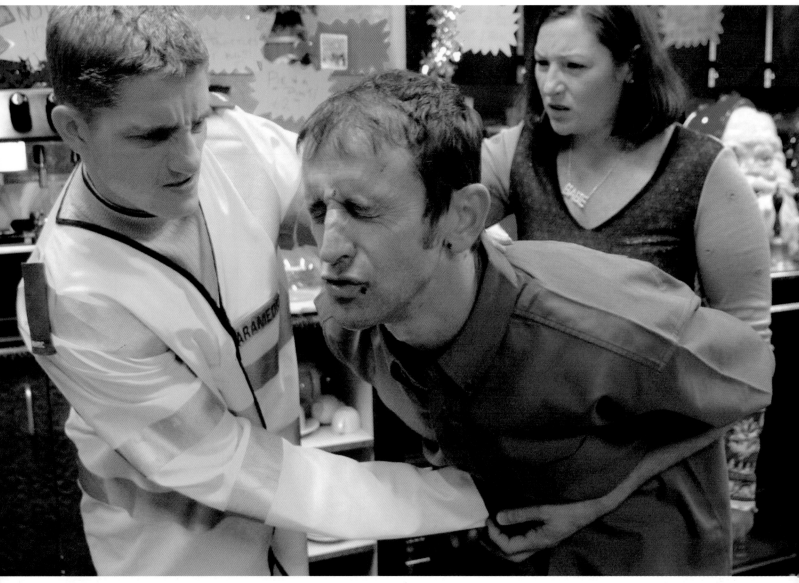

Above: Tim gets revenge on Christie

and even bookish, was unlike former potential teenage-mothers depicted in the programme.

Katy Lamont, who plays Adele, remembers when the pregnancy was first broached to her: '*Brookside* spoke to my mum and me, and asked if she would be happy with me playing this part and the storyline. I was really excited – it was a new challenge.'

With her stepmother desperate for a child of her own, the debate about whether Adele should keep the baby or not gained an extra edge.

Adele and Leo get friendly

TRIBUTES

This year *Brookside* was paid two notable tributes. First, on May 21, Phil Redmond picked up a Special Achievement award at the Soap Awards, reflecting the continuing success of *Brookside* since 1982 (and latterly, *Hollyoaks*). On receiving the honour he said: 'Remember, it's not the genre, it's what you do with it that counts. This business is about investing in people, their ideas and their intellectual capacities.'

Second, in August, outgoing Series Producer Paul Marquess also had words of praise for the series. 'I'm proud to have played my part in the long and highly eventful life of Britain's best soap,' he said. 'At *Brookside*, it's been my privilege to work with Phil Redmond – and some of the best actors and writers on television. I feel we've upheld the programme's reputation for tackling social issues head on – including child abuse, infertility and teenage pregnancy – while never losing sight of our mission to provide gripping drama. It's a wrench to leave ; *Brookside* has a habit of getting under your skin.'

Lindsey Corkhill

REACTION

On March 9, six celebrities entered television's infamous *Big Brother* house to raise money for the charity 'Comic Relief'. One of their number was Claire Sweeney (Lindsey Corkhill). The production team on *Brookside* had originally said a firm no to losing a cast member out of the carefully planned and heavy schedules at relatively short notice for such a long period of time. But Phil Redmond was fully supportive of the idea and ensured the schedule was cleared.

Over the next seven days the heightened attention on Sweeney saw the public take the actress to their heart, thanks to her sense of humour and genuine character. Writing for *The Guardian* at the time, a contestant from the previous year's *Big Brother*, Nick Bateman, commented favourably on how 'real' Sweeney was behaving. *Scotland on Sunday* newspaper agreed, saying: '[Claire] hit the big time simply by being herself in the *Big Brother* house.'

Later in the year, Sweeney moved on from *Brookside* to host the ITV1 programme *Challenge of a Lifetime* and then went on to enjoy success in the West End musical *Chicago*. Writing for *The Guardian*, Gareth McLean – for one – missed her, feeling that 'the sun is a little lower in the wide Merseyside sky' since Lindsey Corkhill left the Close.

Towards the end of the year all eyes were on the plight of Ron Dixon as he stood trial for the shooting of Clint Moffat. Talking to *Inside Soap* magazine, actor Vince Earl enthused '[The storyline] has captured viewers' imaginations.' Meanwhile *Heat* magazine featured the trial episodes as one of their picks of the week. 'The real [drama], of course, happens in Friday's episode,' it wrote, 'but we'd advise you to be in on this one from the start.'

Top: Anthony Murray is victimised; Bottom: Imelda Clough, bullying Anthony

BROOKSIDE: Episodes 2641 –
WRITERS: Maurice Bessman, Roy Boulter, Peter Cox, Arthur Ellison,
John Fay, Tom Higgins, Neil Jones, Andy Lynch, Jan McVerry,
Sue Mooney, Carmel Morgan, Heather Robson,
Trea Smallcombe, Barry Woodward, David Young

DIRECTORS: Vernon Antcliff, Adrian Bean, Darrol Blake, Chris Corcoran,
Steve Finn, Maurice Hutchinson, Nigel Keen, James Larkin, Daikin Marsh,
Paul Murphy, David Richardson, Peter Rose, Mark Sendell, Jeremy Summers,
Patrick Tucker, Ali Turnbull, Luke Watson

TRANSMISSION: January 2 –

2002

HOUSE BY HOUSE

5 The Gordons arrive in the middle of the year to start a new life in Brookside Close. Ruth shocks the family, telling them she's left her husband Sean Smith. She reveals she's now seeing her ex-boyfriend Dan Morrisey.

6 Helen from the bingo tracks Ray down and reveals she's his daughter. Jessie falls out with Ray over the skeletons in his cupboard, but when he tries to make amends with a romantic candle-lit evening the bungalow is set on fire. Jerome is almost killed in the blaze. Ray and Jessie move into No.8 as lodgers.

7 Jacqui finds out she is pregnant and has mixed feelings. She gets caught up in a car accident, but is relatively unhurt. Later she collapses in the Parade and loses her baby due to an ectopic pregnancy. Max agrees to a house swap with the Dixons.

8 The Hiltons discover they're under-insured for No.6 and can't reimburse Nikki and Jerome for everything they've lost. Mike and Rachel go to court over their debts. Ron returns home to find his house is full. Dr Gary Parr fails to diagnose Beth's meningitis, and Mike swears revenge. Ron collapses with a heart attack. A by-pass is needed and he is adamant he'll wait for it on the NHS.

9 The school excludes Imelda and the Murrays are hopeful that Anthony's hell is over. However she still continues to harass Anthony and in a struggle she drowns in a pond. The police question Marty about Imelda's disappearance and Anthony begins to convince himself that Marty actually killed her. Marty reveals to Diane that he's got a record for hitting his ex-wife, Jan.

10 Ignoring his doctor's advice, Jimmy comes off his medication. Tim and Steve plan a heist, but an increasingly erratic Jimmy tags along, almost getting caught but then escaping in a dumper truck. Jimmy walks through the Mersey tunnel causing more concern for his mental health. Nikki decides to become Jimmy's carer, and he starts taking his medication again. Jimmy gets together with Helen but Nikki is concerned she's unrealistic about his condition. Nikki agrees to marry Jerome and Helen's mother arrives on the Close. Tim tells Steve he's planning a bank job.

The fire at No. 6

Ron's released

Anthony's been attacked

In confession

151

THE PARADE

Bev returns to find that Leanne's run her bar into the ground. Katie grows more dependent on alcohol. Bev and Jimmy share a night of passion on the pool table in Bev's Bar. Leanne seeks revenge and smashes up the bar, so Bev attacks her in retaliation. Jacqui announces she is going to buy Bev's Bar and rename it Bar Brookie. Steve runs over Josh who suffers a broken leg. Rob Dexter arrives on the Close and starts harassing the Parrs. When Gabby spurns him he commits suicide.

'I'M BACK'

Not long before Christmas 2001, Phil Redmond chaired a meeting in the Bev's Bar set at Mersey Television. From *Brookside's* newly appointed Senior Producer, David Hanson, through the whole cast, to the editor of the Brookside website – everyone connected with the programme was there. With various rumours circulating in the press about the programme's direction, it was time to clear the air.

Redmond confirmed that there were going to be changes at the top, but that these were really only tantamount to one thing. 'I'm back,' he said. In order to take *Brookside* through its twentieth year on screen, Redmond had decided that he was going to take a more hands-on approach with the programme again. It was not that he had ever really been away, however, having always attended long-term storyline meetings and remaining the public face of *Brookside*. It was

just that in 2002, Redmond was going to involve himself in every aspect of the programme's production again. It was going to be like the old days.

THE BULLYING OF ANTHONY MURRAY

Brookside's year 20 finds the programme as ever exploring a vast range of thought provoking and challenging subjects. An early high-water mark has already been reached with the unravelling of the Anthony Murray storyline.

On March 6, Mersey Television issued a press release which said: '*Brookside* is back tackling difficult social issues! This time it is bullying and a harrowing storyline that will take viewers on a dramatic journey into uncompromising territory to witness a child killed by another child. Celebrating its 20th anniversary in November, *Brookside* prides itself on producing thought-provoking drama and through this latest storyline is firmly underlining its credentials as an issue-led programme. The climax of this story is what... Phil Redmond saw as following bullying to one of two ultimate conclusions – either the death of the victim or the perpetrator.'

Redmond himself added to this release by saying: 'Like many big *Brookside* storylines, this is not the end of a story, but merely the beginning of the next phase. Although the death of the bully, Imelda, is tragic in its own right, we will be following our central character Anthony and how he deals with this terrible turn of events and later, how his family cope. For every parent it is one of the dark horrors you push

away from your mind every day, the discovery that the child you love has found themselves in such horrific circumstances.

David Hanson, for one, is extremely proud of this story: 'For thousands of children, their school days are made miserable because of bullying – and we wanted to reflect the truth of the situation, not only for the bullied children but also their families, who often feel powerless to do anything about the problem.'

He continued: 'The twist in our tale came when Anthony finally snapped and struggled with Imelda, accidentally killing her. This gave us the opportunity to spin the story in a totally new direction – and to explore the impact that such a shocking event would have on a child and the child's family.'

The quality of the storyline and the accomplished performance of Raymond Quinn, who plays Anthony Murray, were reflected in this year's Soap Awards where *Brookside* won the Best Storyline award, whilst Quinn took the Best Performance prize. Hanson comments that 'it is to the credit of the Murray family, but especially young Raymond Quinn, that the storyline has been as affecting as it has.' He also reveals that, 'there's a long way to go – and the story is again going to spin off in a new direction.'

THE NEW LOOK

In addition to depicting Imelda's death, the March 20 edition of *Brookside* was historic for another reason as the programme adopted a new look. With this episode *Brookside* went 'filmic',

Gabby and Gary Parr

a post-production process which alters the video the programme is shot on to give it the richer, glossier quality of film. The process, which has been used on Mersey Television's *Hollyoaks* since 1995, was trialled on *Brookside's* 2001 Christmas special and considered such a success that from 2002 it has become a fixed part of the programme's look. 'It has been popular with some viewers, unpopular with others,' says Hanson, 'but we feel that it gives our drama a more immediate quality.'

PRODUCING BROOKSIDE: DAVID HANSON

David Hanson was born in Chorlton, Manchester in 1957. His first job was for an import/export company, troubleshooting cargo through the docks at Salford.

After studying at Salford University, Hanson responded to an advert in the *Manchester Evening News* in 1979 to work in the Script Department at Granada Television.

From there he progressed to the role of Producer working on the soap operas *Revelations*, *Springhill*, *Castles*, the feature length *Coronation Street* video release and the regular programme itself. He also produced the courtroom drama, *Verdict*.

Hanson joined *Brookside* in March 2001 as a Producer, becoming Senior Producer in August 2001.

THE FUTURE

Barry Woodward, who has been writing for *Brookside* since it started, says of his time on the programme: 'I've loved all of it,' and goes on to add: 'The show is in my blood after all these years, and I find it as interesting to write for now as back in the eighties and nineties.'

As *Brookside* moves through its anniversary and beyond, it is set to mark this superb achievement with one of the most dramatic storylines in the programme's history. With recent 'must see' and 'compelling' notices from the *Daily Mirror* and *The Liverpool Echo*, *Brookside* is setting out on its next 20 years with the same ambition, determination and quality that marked its debut in 1982.

The Gordons: Debbie, Alan, Stuart, Kirsty, Ali and Ruth

REGULAR CHARACTERS

Character name (actor's name) first – last appearance

CARL BANKS (Stephen Donald) 1994–95. Son of **Rosie** and **Eddie**, brother to **Lee**, and father to Rebecca, he was unfaithful to wife **Sarah** with **Margaret Clemence** and **Jacqui Dixon**, before leaving for Dubai.

EDDIE BANKS (Paul Broughton) 1994–96. Husband of **Rosie**, and father to **Carl** and **Lee**, he had an affair with daughter-in-law **Sarah**, before leaving the Close for a new start with Rosie.

LEE BANKS (Matthew Lewney) 1994–96. Son of **Rosie** and **Eddie**, and brother to **Carl**, teenage joyrider Lee came to the Close after serving two years in a young offenders' institution.

ROSIE BANKS (Susan Twist) 1994–96. Wife of **Eddie**, and mother to **Carl** and **Lee**, sister of Mo McGee her gambling addiction lost the family home.

SARAH BANKS (Andrea Marshall) 1994–96. Wife of **Carl**, and mother to Rebecca, her husband's infidelity drove her to a brief affair with father-in-law, **Eddie**, before leaving the Close.

MARCIA BARRETT (Cheryl Maiker) 1990–93. Ex-girlfriend of **Ellis Johnson**, she got engaged to **Sinbad** but dramatically called off the wedding at the last minute.

NISHA BATRA (Sunetra Sarker) 1988– . Teenage friend to **Sammy Rogers**, she returned to work as a nurse in the Doctor's surgery.

HEATHER BLACK (née Haversham, formerly Huntington) (Amanda Burton) 1982–86. Wife of **Nicholas**, previously married to **Roger Huntington**, she was a career woman who left the Close when Nicholas died of a heroin overdose.

NICHOLAS BLACK (Alan Rothwell) 1985–86. Divorced from Barbara, and father to Scott, Ruth and Adam, he married **Heather**. Best friend, Charlie Dawson, supplied him with heroin, which eventually led to his death.

CHERYL BOYANOWSKY (Jennifer Calvert) 1988–89. A Canadian student, she met **Jonathan Gordon-Davies** on a ski-ing holiday in Austria and lived with him after the death of his wife, Laura.

ANNE BRADLEY (Faith Brown) 1996. Wife of **JC Bradley**, and mother to **Jules**, she enjoyed looking down on the Simpsons' reduced circumstances.

JC BRADLEY (Ken Sharrock) 1996–97. Husband of Anne, and father to **Jules**, he hounded **Nat** and **Georgia Simpson** out of Merseyside after discovering their incestuous relationship.

JULES BRADLEY (Sarah Withe) 1996. Daughter of **Anne** and **JC**, she married **Nat Simpson** but took an overdose when she found out about his incestuous relationship with sister **Georgia Simpson**.

ANTHEA BRINDLEY – see Anthea Dixon

JULIA BROGAN (Gladys Ambrose) 1985–98. Widow of Arthur, and mother to **Doreen Corkhill**, she worked for **Ron Dixon** in The Trading Post and **Jacqui Dixon** in the hairdressers. She was let down in love by Ron's bigamous father **Cyril Dixon**, and **Terry's** father, Jack Sullivan.

KIRSTY BROWN (Joanne Black) 1986–89. Nagging girlfriend of **Rod Corkhill**, she dumped him after his affair with WPC Emma Reid and took up with his best friend, PC Neil Thompson.

CASSIE CHARLTON (Ebony Gray) 1996–98. Daughter of **Gladys**, and sister of **Elaine Davies**, she reported Elaine and **Mick Johnson** to the police after they assisted a terminally ill Gladys to end her life.

GLADYS CHARLTON (Eileen O'Brien) 1996–97. Mother to **Cassie** and **Elaine Davies**, she refused treatment for her terminal cancer and persuaded Elaine and boyfriend **Mick Johnson** to help her end her life.

CAROLINE CHOI (Sarah Lam) 1989–90. Daughter of Stephen, and sister to **Michael**, she left the Close after her ex-boyfriend James Markham embezzled from her business.

DR MICHAEL CHOI (David Yip) 1989–90. Son of Stephen, and brother to **Caroline**, his first priority was daughter Jessica. He left for a new life in America.

MARGARET CLEMENCE (Nicola Stephenson) 1990–94. Nanny to **Max** and **Patricia Farnham's** son Thomas, she had a relationship with Father **Derek O'Farrell**. After a brief lesbian liaison with **Beth Jordache**, Margaret joined Derek in Bosnia.

ANNABELLE COLLINS (Doreen Sloane) 1982–90. Wife of **Paul**, and mother to **Gordon** and **Lucy**, she had an affair with fellow magistrate **Brian Lawrence** before moving to the Lake District to care for her mother, **Mona Fallon**.

GORDON COLLINS (Nigel Crowley/Mark Burgess) 1982–90. Son of **Annabelle** and **Paul**, and brother to **Lucy**, his parents were shocked to learn he was gay.

LUCY COLLINS (Katrin Cartlidge/Maggie Saunders) 1982–90. Daughter of **Annabelle** and **Paul**, and sister to **Gordon**, she had an affair with a married man before departing permanently for France.

PAUL COLLINS (Jim Wiggins) 1982–90. Husband of **Annabelle**, and father to **Gordon** and **Lucy**, his redundancy led to the family moving to Brookside Close.

BILLY CORKHILL (John McArdle) 1985–90. Husband of **Doreen**, and later **Sheila**, father to **Rod** and **Tracy**, and brother to **Jimmy** and Frankie, his time on the Close was marked by a descent into debt and crime before he left with Sheila and her daughter Claire for a new start in Basingstoke.

DIANA CORKHILL (née Spence) (Paula Frances) 1990–93. Wife of **Rod**, she overcame her illiteracy but split with Rod and was raped by **Peter Harrison**, whose not guilty verdict left her feeling betrayed and vulnerable.

DOREEN CORKHILL (Kate Fitzgerald) 1985–90. Wife of **Billy**, mother to **Rod** and **Tracy**, and daughter of **Julia Brogan**, Doreen got the family into huge debts and left after finding out about Billy's criminal activities.

JACKIE CORKHILL (Sue Jenkins) 1991–2001. Wife of **Jimmy**, and mother to **Lindsey**, **Little Jimmy** and William, she had a half-hearted affair with **Ron Dixon**, and was pursued by Lindsey's lesbian lover Shelley, but generally stuck by Jimmy until they separated.

JIMMY CORKHILL (Dean Sullivan) 1985– . Husband of **Jackie**, father to **Lindsey**, **Little Jimmy** and William, and brother to **Billy** and Frankie, he descended from lovable rogue to hardened criminal and drug addict, only to reform and train as a teacher, but lost his job after the onset of bipolar disorder.

LITTLE JIMMY CORKHILL (George Christopher) 1991–96. Son of **Jackie** and **Jimmy**, and brother to **Lindsey**, he became a drug addict and was executed by dealers he owed money to.

LINDSEY CORKHILL (Claire Sweeney) 1991–2001. Daughter of **Jackie** and **Jimmy**, and mother to Kylie, Lindsey left husband **Gary Stanlow**, and had relationships with **Mike Dixon**, **Barry Grant** and married **Peter Phelan**, before having a lesbian relationship with Shelley.

ROD CORKHILL (Jason Hope) 1985–93. Son of **Doreen** and **Billy**, and brother to **Tracy**, he was engaged to **Kirsty Black**, before marrying **Diana Spence**. After sustaining an injury in the course of his police work he left Diana to start a new life in Hull.

SHEILA CORKHILL – see Sheila Grant

TRACY CORKHILL (Justine Kerrigan) 1985–92. Daughter of **Doreen** and **Billy**, and sister to **Rod**, she slept with **Barry Grant** to spite her father for taking up with **Sheila Grant**, but became pregnant and had a termination.

DAVID CROSBIE (John Burgess) 1992–98. Husband of **Jean**, and father to **Patricia Farnham**, he had an affair with **Audrey Manners**, and moved in with Molly Marchbank after Jean left him.

JEAN CROSBIE (Marcia Ashton) 1992–96. Wife of **David**, and mother to **Patricia Farnham**, she moved to France after David confessed his affair, shortly joined by Patricia.

PENNY CROSBIE (Mary Tamm) 1993–95. Sister-in-law to **David**, she was widowed when husband Clive, David's MP brother, committed suicide to avoid a sex scandal. She had an affair with **Barry Grant** before leaving the Close.

EDNA CROSS (Betty Alberge) 1983–85. Wife of **Harry**, mother to **Kevin**, she left Harry devastated when she died of a stroke.

HARRY CROSS (Bill Dean) 1983–90. Husband of **Edna**, father to Kevin, an old curmudgeon who grew to depend on his lodger **Ralph Hardwick**, and moved to St Helen's when Ralph remarried.

GRAEME CURTIS (David Banks) 1985. Became obsessed with **Sue Sullivan**, but killed himself in prison after being wrongly convicted of Sue and her baby Danny's murder.

OWEN DANIELS (Danny McCall) 1989–93. Husband of **Sammy**, father to Louise, they married after discovering Sammy was pregnant, but it was a difficult relationship and they split in 1996.

SAMMY DANIELS (née Rogers) (Rachel Lindsay) 1987–. Ex-wife of **Owen**, separated from Richard, mother to Louise, daughter of **Chrissy** and **Frank**, sister to **Katie** and **Geoff**, she developed an alcohol problem and after the break-up of her marriage returned to the Close in 2001.

ELAINE DAVIES – see Elaine Johnson

ANTHEA DIXON (formerly Brindley) (Barbara Hatwell) 1998–2001. Ex-wife of **Ron** and mother to Megan.

CYRIL DIXON (Allan Surtees) 1990–91. Father to **Ron**, he was a bigamist three times over. Ron disowned him when he found out and Cyril died of a heart attack before they reconciled.

DD DIXON (Irene Marot) 1990–96. Ex-wife of **Ron**, mother to **Mike**, **Jacqui** and **Tony**, staunch Catholic Deborah (known as DD), lost Ron to **Bev McLoughlin**, but found happiness with younger man Tom.

JACQUI DIXON – see Jacqui Farnham

MIKE DIXON (Paul Byatt) 1990–. Husband of **Rachel**, father to Beth (by Rachel) and Josh (by Bev McLoughlin), son of **DD** and **Ron Dixon**, and brother to **Jacqui** and **Tony**, he is one of life's losers with a succession of dead end jobs, and constant money worries.

RACHEL DIXON (née Jordache, formerly Wright) (Tiffany Chapman) 1993–. Wife of **Mike**, mother to Beth, daughter of **Mandy** and **Trevor**, sister to **Beth** and half-sister to Ruth, her father abused her and he was murdered by Mandy and Beth. She had a brief marriage to **Christian Wright**.

RON DIXON (Vince Earl) 1990. Ex-husband of **DD** and **Anthea** and father of **Mike**, **Jacqui**, **Tony** and Megan Brindley, he blew up the parade fitting his own gas cooker, and killed **Katie Rogers'** boyfriend **Clint Moffat** with an illegal shotgun.

TONY DIXON (Gerard Bostock/Mark Lennock) 1990–94. Son of **DD** and **Ron**, brother to **Mike** and **Jacqui**, he was in a coma after **Jimmy Corkhill** crashed into **Frank Rogers'** car, and later died.

MARIANNE DWYER (Jodie Hanson) 1992–94. Initially going out with **Ellis Johnson**, she transferred her affection to his brother **Mick**, but after two abortive wedding days left for Glasgow.

MONA FALLON (previously Harvey) (Margaret Clifton) 1987–89. Mother of **Annabelle Collins**, she was abused in a nursing home before marrying Gerald Fallon and moving to the Lake District.

JACQUI FARNHAM (née Dixon) (Alexandra Fletcher) 1990. Wife of **Max**, mother to Harry, step-mother to Emma, daughter of **DD** and **Ron Dixon**, and sister to **Mike** and **Tony**, a hard-headed businesswoman, she had a surrogate baby for Max and **Susannah**, then married Max after Susannah's death.

MAX FARNHAM (Stephen Pinder) 1990–. Ex-husband of **Susannah** and **Patricia** and married to **Jacqui**, father of Matthew, Emily, Thomas, Alice, Emma and Harry, he accidentally killed Susannah.

PATRICIA FARNHAM (Gabrielle Glaister) 1990–96. Ex-wife of **Max**, mother to Thomas and Alice, she battled against breast cancer before moving to France with her mother, **Jean Crosbie**. She met a new man and moved to Canada.

SUSANNAH FARNHAM – see Susannah Morrisey

ALAN GORDON (John Burton) 2002–. Husband of **Debbie**, father of **Ruth**, **Kirsty**, **Ali** and **Stuart**, Alan is a manager with a haulage firm.

ALI GORDON (Kris Mocherrie) 2002–. Son of **Alan** and **Debbie**, brother to **Ruth**, **Kirsty** and **Stuart**, he was unhappy about the family moving to the Close.

DEBBIE GORDON (Annette Ekblom) 2002–. Wife of **Alan** and mother of **Ruth**, **Kirsty**, **Ali** and **Stuart**, she runs the local garage.

KIRSTY GORDON (Jessica Noon) 2002–. Daughter of **Alan** and **Debbie**, sister to **Ruth**, **Ali** and **Stuart**, she betrayed her family by supporting Manchester United.

STUART GORDON (David Lyon) 2002–. Son of **Alan** and **Debbie**, brother to **Ruth**, **Kirsty** and **Ali**, he is into the internet in a big way.

JONATHAN GORDON-DAVIES (Steven Finch) 1987–90. Husband of **Laura**, he was devastated at her death shortly after their marriage.

LAURA GORDON-DAVIES (née Wright) (Jane Cunliffe) 1987. Wife of **Jonathan**, she died after an accident caused by her father's faulty wiring.

BARRY GRANT (Paul Usher) 1982–98. Son of **Sheila** and **Matty Nolan**, brother to **Karen**, **Damon** and **Claire**, father of Stephen, married to Pam, he was best friends with **Terry Sullivan** until he killed his wife, **Sue** and her baby son Danny. A hard-man, he has a lot of blood on his hands, as well as money and power.

BOBBY GRANT (Ricky Tomlinson) 1982–88. Husband of **Sheila**, and father to **Karen**, **Damon** and Claire, he never knew that **Barry** was not his son.

DAMON GRANT (Simon O'Brien) 1982–87. Son of **Sheila** and **Bobby**, brother to **Barry** and **Karen**, he fell in love with **Debbie McGrath** but was fatally stabbed when they ran away to York.

KAREN GRANT (Shelagh O'Hara) 1982–90. Daughter of **Sheila** and **Bobby**, sister to **Barry**, **Damon** and Claire, she went to university before moving to London.

SHEILA GRANT (Sue Johnston) 1982–90. Wife of **Bobby**, and mother to **Barry**, **Karen**, **Damon** and **Claire**, her guilty secret was that Barry's father was Bobby's best friend, **Matty Nolan**. After the breakdown of her marriage to Bobby, she married **Billy Corkhill** and moved to Basingstoke with him and Claire.

PAT HANCOCK (David Easter) 1984–87. Shared a house with **Kate Moses** and **Sandra Maghie**, and was held hostage by John Clarke.

RALPH HARDWICK (Ray Dunbobbin) 1984–89. Widowed friend of **Harry** and **Edna Cross**, he became their lodger and lived with Harry after Edna's death. Married Lana Costello and retired to the USA.

SUE HARPER – see Sue Sullivan

BARBARA HARRISON (Angela Morant) 1991–93. Wife of **John**, and mother to **Peter**, deputy headteacher at Brookside Comprehensive, she left after Peter was accused of rape.

JOHN HARRISON (Geoffrey Leesley) 1991–93. Husband of **Barbara**, and father to **Peter**, early retirement and the stress of a VAT fraud charge led him to shoplifting.

PETER HARRISON (Robert Beck) 1992–93. Son of **Barbara** and **Peter**, **Diana Corkhill** accused him of rape. He was found not guilty but left for Oxford.

MONA HARVEY – see Mona Fallon

HEATHER HAVERSHAM – see Heather Black

JESSIE HILTON (previously Shadwick) (Marji Campi) 1998–. Wife of **Ray**, mother to **Greg**, almost lost her life when the bungalow caught fire.

RAY HILTON (Kenneth Cope) 1999–. Husband of **Jessie**, son of Kitty, father of Helen, discovered his daughter late in life.

LOUISE HOPE (Lisa Faulkener) 1998. Daughter of **Eleanor Kitson** and Marcus Seddon, she tried to reunite her parents, which ended in his death after taking her, Eleanor and **Ollie** and **Dan Simpson** hostage.

SIMON HOWE (Lee Hartney) 1993–94. Cult leader who indoctrinated **Katie Rogers** and **Terry Sullivan**, before kidnapping **Barry Grant**, blowing up No.5 and committing suicide in Barry's car.

HEATHER HUNTINGTON – see Heather Black

ROGER HUNTINGTON (Rob Spendlove) 1982–83. Husband of **Heather**, he had an affair with his client, Diane McAllister, and Heather threw him out.

GEORGE JACKSON (Cliff Howells) 1983–85. Husband of **Marie**, and father to twins, Gary and Little George, George was framed for a warehouse robbery, and served 18 months in prison.

MARIE JACKSON (Anna Keaveney) 1983–85. Wife of **George**, mother to twins Gary and Little George, sister to **Petra Taylor** and Michelle, she started the 'Free George Jackson' campaign when he was wrongly imprisoned, but was intimidated from the Close.

ELAINE JOHNSON (née Davies) (Beverley Hills) 1996-97. Wife of **Mick**, mother to Tanya, daughter to **Gladys Charlton**, and sister to **Cassie Charlton**, she went on the run after she and Mick assisted Gladys in ending her life.

ELLIS JOHNSON (Francis Johnson) 1991–93. Brother to **Mick**, he succeeded in losing him his livelihood as a cabbie and putting him in deep debt to buy the pizza parlour.

GEMMA JOHNSON (Naomi Kamanga) 1990–2000. Daughter of **Mick** and **Josie**, she lived with Mick until she was hospitalised after taking Ecstasy, then she went to live with Josie.

JEROME JOHNSON (Leon Lopez) 1998– . Nephew of **Mick**, relationship with **Nikki Shadwick** blighted by affair with Nisha Batra.

LEO JOHNSON (Leeon Sawyer/Steven Cole) 1990–2001. Son of **Mick** and **Josie**, Leo joined the police force, but left Liverpool after sleeping with 15-year-old **Adele Murray**.

MICK JOHNSON (Louis Emerick) 1989–2001. Father to **Leo** and **Gemma**, Mick was married to **Josie** and then **Elaine**, and engaged to **Susannah Morrisey** at the time of her death.

MICHELLE JONES (Tracey Jay) 1983–85. Sister of Marie Jackson and Petra Taylor, daughter of Davy Jones, dated Terry Sullivan until she was caught in bed with dancing instructor Richard de Saville.

BETH JORDACHE (Anna Friel) 1993–95. Daughter of **Mandy** and **Trevor**, sister to **Rachel** and Ruth, she helped Mandy kill the abusive Trevor. She went to prison and died from a genetic heart condition.

BRENNA JORDACHE (Gillian Hanna) 1993–95. Sister to **Trevor**, refused to believe that he was abusive to his family, and tried to poison **Mandy Jordache** in vengeance when she was released on appeal.

MANDY JORDACHE (Sandra Maitland) 1993–95. Wife of **Trevor**, mother to **Beth** and **Rachel** (by Trevor) and Ruth (by **Sinbad**), she killed Trevor after years of abuse, and was sent to prison, but released on appeal.

RACHEL JORDACHE – see Rachel Dixon

TREVOR JORDACHE (Bryan Murray) 1993. Husband of **Mandy**, and father to **Beth** and **Rachel**, brother to **Brenna**, he tracked his family to their safe house after his release from prison, and the abuse continued. Desperate, Beth and Mandy killed him.

ELEANOR KITSON (Georgia Reece) 1997–98. Lived with **Ollie Simpson**, and his son **Dan**, was tracked down by the daughter she had given up at birth, **Louise Hope**, who brought her father, Marcus Seddon, back on the scene. After his death, Ollie couldn't forgive her affair and she left.

DEBBIE MCGRATH (Gillian Kearney) 1986–88. Schoolgirl girlfriend of **Damon Grant**, they ran away together to York, where Damon was stabbed. Debbie later gave birth to his son, Simon.

BEV MCLOUGHLIN (Sarah White) 1993– . Sister to **Lyn Rogers**, she wrecked her sister's marriage before splitting up **Ron** and **DD Dixon**. She had an affair with **Mike Dixon**, and had his son Josh. Was in marriage of convenience with Lance Powell's partner, Fred Gonzales.

SANDRA MAGHIE (Sheila Grier) 1984–86. Shared a house with **Kate Moses** and **Pat Hancock**, and was held hostage by John Clarke.

AUDREY MANNERS (Judith Barker) 1994–95. Wife of **George**, she had a fling with **David Crosbie**, before dying from the mystery virus.

GEORGE MANNERS (Brian Murphy) 1995. Husband of **Audrey**, he returned from Kenya with a mystery virus, which swept the Close. He was one of the fatalities.

LYN MATTHEWS – see Lyn Rogers

CLINT MOFFAT (Greg Pateras) 2000–01. Brother of **Robbie**, boyfriend of **Katie Rogers**, accidentally killed by **Ron Dixon**.

ROBBIE MOFFAT (Neil Davies) 2000–01. Brother of **Clint**, bad boy, went out with **Jacqui Dixon**, and terrorised **Ron Dixon**.

SUSANNAH MORRISEY (Karen Drury) 1991–2000. Ex-wife of **Max Farnham**, mother to Matthew, Emily and Emma, she married Max twice, and had surrogate baby Harry (by **Jacqui Dixon**) and Emma with Max, after Matthew and Emily died in a car crash. Susannah died when she fell down stairs, arguing with Max.

KATE MOSES (Sharon Rosita) 1984–85. Shared a house with **Pat Hancock** and **Sandra Maghie**, she was held hostage by John Clarke, who killed her before turning his gun on himself.

ADELE MURRAY (Katy Lamont) 2000– . Daughter of **Marty**, sister to **Steve** and **Anthony**, she had a termination after becoming pregnant by **Leo Johnson**, despite opposition from step-mother **Diane**.

ANTHONY MURRAY (Raymond Quinn) 2000– . Son of **Marty**, brother to **Steve** and **Adele**, stepson to **Diane**, in desperation he killed Imelda who had been bullying him at school.

CHRISTY MURRAY (Glynn Pritchard) 2000– . Brother of **Marty**, had a relationship with **Leanne Powell**.

DIANE MURRAY (Bernie Nolan) 2000– . Wife of **Marty**, step-mother to **Steven**, **Adele** and **Anthony**, and daughter of Brigid, she tried IVF to have her own baby.

MARTY MURRAY (Neil Caple) 2000– . Husband of **Diane**, father to **Steven**, **Adele** and **Anthony**, a suspect in Imelda's murder.

STEVEN MURRAY (Stephen Fletcher) 2000 . Son of **Marty**, brother to **Anthony** and **Adele**, step-son to **Diane**, pulled various scams with **Tim O'Leary**.

JOEY MUSGROVE (Dan Mullane) 1998–2000. Husband of **Niamh**, and father to **Luke**, **Ryan**, **Matt** and **Kelly**, he lost his job as a taxi-driver due to drink problems.

KELLY MUSGROVE (Natalie Earl) 1998–2000. Daughter of **Joey** and **Niamh**, sister to **Luke**, **Ryan** and **Matt** she was friends with **Leo Johnson** and **Tim O'Leary**.

LUKE MUSGROVE (Jason Kavanagh) 1998–2000. Son of **Joey** and **Niamh**, brother to **Ryan**, **Matt** and **Kelly**, he was brought up in Ireland and drug-raped **Nikki Shadwick**.

MATT MUSGROVE (Cristian Ealey) 1998–2000. Son of **Joey** and **Niamh**, brother to **Ryan**, **Luke** and **Kelly**, he planted cannabis in the house.

NIAMH MUSGROVE (Barbara Drennan) 1998–2000. Wife of **Joey**, and mother to **Luke**, **Ryan**, **Matt** and **Kelly**, she revealed she was illiterate.

RYAN MUSGROVE (Sam Hudson) 1998–2000. Son of **Joey** and **Niamh**, brother to **Luke**, **Matt** and **Kelly**, father to Lia, he worked as a taxi-driver.

MATTY NOLAN (Tony Scoggo) 1982–92. Best friend of **Bobby Grant**, and **Barry Grant's** real father. Wife Teresa committed suicide when he was questioned about the rape of **Sheila Grant**.

DEREK O'FARRELL (Clive Moore) 1990–94. Brother to **DD Dixon**, a Catholic priest, he had a relationship with **Margaret Clemence** before giving up the priesthood.

BEN O'LEARY (Simon Paul) 1997–98. Son of **Carmel**, and brother to **Tim** and **Melanie**, he suffered permanent spinal injuries in the gas explosion.

CARMEL O'LEARY (Carol Connor) 1996–2000. Single mother to **Ben**, **Tim** and **Melanie**, her relationship with **Sinbad** ended when she found out about his part in the gas explosion.

EMILY O'LEARY (née Shadwick) (Jennifer Ellison) 1998–. Wife of **Tim**, daughter of **Margi** and **Greg**, and sister to **Nikki** and **Jason**, she determined to avenge Susannah's part in the death of her father. Married **Tim O'Leary** in 2001.

MELANIE O'LEARY (Elizabeth Lovelady) 1997–98. Daughter of **Carmel**, and sister to **Ben** and **Tim**, she had a lucky escape when Tim's firework sent a lorry crashing into their house.

TIM O'LEARY (Tinhead) (Philip Olivier) 1996–. Husband of **Emily**, son of **Carmel**, and brother to **Ben** and **Melanie**, he was a bully at school, and despite his good side, has descended into a life of crime, and has been to prison.

ALAN PARTRIDGE (Dicken Ashworth) 1983–84. A computer expert, he eventually married his girlfriend **Sam**, and moved to Kuwait.

SAMANTHA PARTRIDGE (Dinah May) 1983–84. A blonde leggy ex-model, she jilted **Alan** at the altar before they finally got married and moved to Kuwait.

FRAN PEARSON (Julie Peasgood) 1991–93. Worked with **Sue Sullivan**, through whom she met **Barry Grant**. She had his baby, Stephen, and fled to Greece to get away from him.

PETER PHELAN (Samuel Kane) 1995–99. Son of Fee, business partner in **Jacqui Dixon**'s hairdressers, he enjoyed a close friendship with **Bev McLoughlin**, much to **Ron Dixon**'s disquiet, before a short-lived marriage to **Lindsey Corkhill**.

LANCE POWELL (Mickey Poppins) 2000–. Brother of **Leanne**, **Bev McLoughlin** married his lover, Fred Gonzales, so he could stay in the country.

LEANNE POWELL (Vickie Gates) 1992–. Sister of **Lance**, she served three years in prison for attacking **Jacqui Dixon**. Returned to work in Bev's Bar in 2000.

DR DARREN ROEBUCK (Timothy Deenihan) 1999–2001. Son of Carolyn, he had an affair with **Susannah Morrisey**, but finally left Brookside with **Victoria Seagram**.

CHRISSY ROGERS (Eithne Browne) 1987–93. Ex-wife of **Frank** and mother to **Sammy**, **Katie** and **Geoff**, she married young and left the Close during Sammy's wedding to **Owen Daniels** to fulfil her thwarted dreams.

FRANK ROGERS (Peter Christian) 1987–93. Husband of **Lyn**, father to **Sammy**, **Katie** and **Geoff**, he remarried after Chrissy left him, but was killed by Jimmy Corkhill on the way to his wedding reception.

GEOFF ROGERS (Kevin Carson/Stephen Walters) 1987–93. Son of **Chrissy** and **Frank**, and brother to **Sammy** and **Katie**, his dyslexia caused problems at school, and despite early promise, he failed to make the grade as a professional footballer.

KATIE ROGERS (Debbie Reynolds/Diane Burke) 1987–. Daughter of **Chrissy** and **Frank**, and sister to **Sammy** and **Geoff**, she was seduced by cult leader **Simon Howe**, developed bulimia, and eventually fell out with best friend **Jacqui Dixon**, when Jacqui's father **Ron** killed her boyfriend **Clint Moffat**.

LYN ROGERS (née McLoughlin, formerly Matthews) (Sharon Power) 1992–94. Wife of **Frank**, sister to **Bev**, mother to Gavin and Alison, her first marriage to Steve ended when he slept with Bev. Following a scuffle with Sammy, she miscarried Frank's baby after his death.

SAMMY ROGERS – see Sammy Daniels.

VICTORIA SEAGRAM (formerly Wilcox) (Patricia Potter) 1999–2001. Married to Mark, a Motor Neurones sufferer who died after falling down a flight of stars, she had a relationship with **Dr Darren Roebuck**.

EMILY SHADWICK – see Emily O'Leary

GREG SHADWICK (Mark Moraghan) 1998–99. Husband of **Margi**, father to **Jason**, **Nikki** and **Emily**, he had an affair with **Susannah Morrisey**, and died in an explosion at the Millennium Club.

JASON SHADWICK (Vincent Price) 1998–2000. Son of **Margi** and **Greg**, and brother to **Nikki** and **Emily**, he died trying to rescue his father in the Millennium Club explosion.

JESSIE SHADWICK – see Jessie Hilton

MARGI SHADWICK (Bernadette Foley) 1998. Wife of **Greg**, and mother to **Jason**, **Nikki** and **Emily**, she left for Brussels in the wake of Greg's death.

NIKKI SHADWICK (Suzanne Collins) 1998–. Daughter of **Margi** and **Greg**, sister to **Jason** and **Emily**, she was raped by **Luke Musgrove**.

BEL SIMPSON (Lesley Nightingale) 1996–97. Wife of **Ollie**, and mother to **Nat**, **Georgia**, and **Danny**, she lost her job after a sexual harassment case, and accused Ollie of abusing Georgia after finding out about Nat and Georgia's incestuous relationship.

DANNY SIMPSON (Andrew Butler) 1996–98. Son of **Bel** and **Ollie**, brother to **Nat** and **Georgia**, led astray by **Tim O'Leary** and forged **Jimmy Corkhill**'s qualifications.

GEORGIA SIMPSON (Helen Grace) 1996–97. Daughter of **Bel** and **Ollie**, sister to **Nat** and **Danny**, she left with Nat after the publicity about their incestuous affair.

JULES SIMPSON – see Jules Bradley

NAT SIMPSON (John Sandford) 1996–97. Son of **Bel** and **Ollie**, brother to **Georgia** and **Nat**, he left wife **Jules** to live incestuously with his sister Georgia.

OLLIE SIMPSON (Michael J. Jackson) 1996–1998. Husband of **Bel**, father to **Nat**, **Georgia** and **Danny**, after his marriage ended he lived with **Eleanor Kitson**, and daughter **Louise**, but ended up being held hostage by her father, Marcus Seddon.

SINBAD (Thomas HE Sweeney) (Michael Starke) 1984–2000. Adopted as a child, he found his real mother Ruth, and named his daughter, by **Mandy Jordache**, after her. He left the Close for a new life after false claims of sexual abuse showed him who his real friends were.

RUTH SMITH (née Gordon) (Lyndsey McCaffrey) 2002–. Daughter of **Alan** and **Debbie**, sister to **Kirsty**, **Ali** and **Stuart**, mother to **Luke**, separated from husband Sean, she is in a relationship with her old boyfriend Dan.

DIANA SPENCE – see Diana Corkhill

GARY STANLOW (Andrew Fillis) 1995–98. Husband of **Lindsey**, and father to Kylie, he enjoyed harassing Lindsey long after their marriage was over, until she threatened to get rid of him, permanently.

LINDSEY STANLOW – see Lindsey Corkhill

SUE SULLIVAN (née Harper) (Annie Miles) 1987–91. Wife of **Terry**, mother to Daniel, she two-timed Terry with **Barry Grant**, who pushed her and Danny off scaffolding, killing them both.

TERRY SULLIVAN (Brian Regan) 1982–97. Husband of **Sue**, he reconciled with her after finding out that he wasn't Danny's father. Devastated by their deaths he was easy prey for cult leader **Simon Howe**, but best friend **Barry Grant** saved him from committing suicide.

GAVIN TAYLOR (Daniel Webb) 1982–83. Husband of **Petra**, he died of a brain haemorrhage.

PETRA TAYLOR (Alexandra Pigg) 1982–83. Wife of **Gavin**, she became depressed after his death and her subsequent miscarriage, and committed suicide.

ANNA WOLSKA (Kazia Pelka) 1992–93. After being fired from her nanny job by **Patricia Farnham**, she drifted into prostitution, and was deported before her arranged marriage to **Terry Sullivan**.

CHRISTIAN WRIGHT (Philip Dowd) 1995–97. Ex-husband of **Rachel**, he became increasingly controlling and abusive, pushing Rachel to consider killing him, but eventually leaving him.

RACHEL WRIGHT – see Rachel Dixon

LAURA WRIGHT – see Laura Gordon-Davies

BROOKSIDE CLOSE RESIDENTS 1982–2002

No.5

The Grants 1982–1989

The Rogers 1989–1994

The Cult 1994

Barry Grant 1994

Carl and Sarah Banks 1995

Mick Johnson and Sinbad 1995–1997

Mick Johnson 1997–2001

The Gordons 2002–

No.6

Alan and Samantha Partridge 1982–1984

The Crosses 1984–1985

Harry Cross and Ralph Hardwick 1985–1989

The Johnsons 1990–1993

The Crosbies 1993–1995

Jacqui Dixon, Katie Rogers and Rachel Jordache 1995–1997

Ron Dixon and David Crosbie 1997–1998

The Shadwicks 1998–2000

The Hiltons 2001–

No.7

The Crosses 1983–1984

Sandra Maghie, Kate Moses and Pat Hancock 1984–1985

Sandra Maghie, Pat Hancock and Terry Sullivan 1985–1987

The Rogers 1987–1989

The Chois 1989–1990

The Farnhams (Max and Patricia) 1990–1996

The Farnhams (Max and Susannah) 1996–2000

Susannah Morrisey 2000

Max Farnham 2001

The Farnhams (Max and Jacqui) 2001–2002

The Dixons 2002–

No.8

The Collins 1982–1990

The Dixons 1990–1993

Ron Dixon and Bev McLoughlin 1993–1997

The O'Learys 1997–1998

The Musgroves 1998–2000

The Dixons 2000–2002

The Farnhams (Max and Jacqui) 2002–

No.9

The Huntingtons 1982–1983

Heather Haversham 1983–1986

The Blacks 1986

Jonathan Gordon-Davies and Laura Wright 1987

Jonathan Gordon-Davies and Terry Sullivan 1987–1990

The Sullivans 1990–1992

The Harrisons 1992–1994

The Banks 1994–1996

The Simpsons 1996–1998

Ollie Simpson and Eleanor Kitson 1998–1999

Lindsey Corkhill 1999–2000

The Murrays 2000–

No.10

The Taylors 1982–1983

The Jacksons 1983–1985

Terry Sullivan and Michelle Jones 1985

The Corkhills (Billy and family) 1985–1993

The Jordaches 1993–1995

The Corkhills (Jimmy and family) 1995–

BIRTHS

January 1985 – Claire, to Sheila and Bobby Grant

December 1988 – Simon, to Debbie McGrath and Damon Grant

September 1989 – Daniel, to Sue Sullivan and Martin Howes

June 1992 – Louise, to Sammy and Owen Daniels

May to November 1992 – Stephen, to Fran Pearson and Barry Grant

December 1993 – Josh, to Bev McLoughlin and Mike Dixon

August 1994 – Alice, to Patricia and Max Farnham

October 1995 – Ruth, to Mandy Jordache and Sinbad

July 1997 – William, to Jackie and Jimmy Corkhill

September 1998 – Harry, to Jacqui Dixon and Max Farnham

January 1999 – Emma, to Susannah Morissey and Max Farnham

December 1999 – Beth, to Rachel Jordache and Mike Dixon

MARRIAGES

July 1984 – Sam to Alan Partridge

June 1986 – Heather Haversham to Nicholas Black

August 1987 – Laura Wright to Jonathan Gordon-Davies

April 1989 – Mona Harvey to Gerald Fallon

August 1989 – Sue Harper to Terry Sullivan

August 1990 – Sheila Grant to Billy Corkhill

November 1991 – Sammy Rogers to Owen Daniels

July 1992 – Diana Spence to Rod Corkhill

October 1993 – Patricia Farnham to Max Farnham

November 1993 – Lyn Matthews to Frank Rogers

August 1996 – Jules Bradley to Nat Simpson

April 1997 – Elaine Davies to Mick Johnson

July 1997 – Rachel Jordache to Christian Wright

July 1998 – Susannah Morisey to Max Farnham

November 1998 – Lindsey Corkhill to Peter Phelan

July 1999 – Anthea Brindley to Ron Dixon

May 2000 – Rachel Jordache to Mike Dixon

January 2001 – Jessie Shadwick to Ray Hilton

February 2001 – Bev McLoughlin to Fred Gonzales

May 2001 – Emily Shadwick to Tim O'Leary

September 2001 – Jacqui Dixon to Max Farnham

DEATHS

February 1983 – Gavin Taylor, brain haemorrhage

January 1984 – Petra Taylor, suicide

November 1984 – Grace Hardwick, natural causes

August 1985 – Kate Moses and John Clarke, shot during the siege

September 1985 – Edna Cross, stroke

August 1986 – Teresa Nolan, suicide

December 1986 – Harriet Haynes, granddaughter of Harry Cross, premature birth

December 1986 – Nick Black, heroin overdose

March 1987 – Lucky the dog, run over by Gordon Collins and Christopher Duncan

November 1987 – Damon Grant, stabbed by unknown assailant

January 1988 – Laura Gordon-Davies, electric shock/fall

December 1988 – Rommel, Ralph Hardwick's dog, poisonous cuddly seal sold by Barry and Terry

April 1990 – James Markham, car crash

May 1990 – Liam Riley, suicide

October 1991 – Sue and Daniel Sullivan, murdered by Barry Grant

December 1991 – Cyril Dixon, heart attack

January 1992 – Graeme Curtis, suicide

May 1993 – Trevor Jordache, stabbed by Mandy Jordache

October 1993 – Clive Crosbie, suicide

November 1993 – Frank Rogers, car crash

February 1994 – Tony Dixon, car crash

October 1994 – Simon Howe, suicide

March 1995 – Gary Salter, Audrey Manners and George Manners, mystery virus

July 1995 – Beth Jordache, heart condition

January 1996 – Shane Cochrane, uncut heroin

November 1996 – Little Jimmy Corkhill, murdered by drug dealers

April 1997 – Matthew and Emily Farnham, car crash

July 1997 – Gladys Charlton, smothered (assisted death)

December 1997 – Cracker, Jimmy Corkhill's dog, killed by a van

September 1998 – Marcus Seddon, fell off a cliff

August 1999 – Greg Shadwick, blown up in the Millennium Club

August 1999 – Jason Shadwick, crushed in the rubble of the Millennium Club

November 2000 – Susannah Morissey, pushed downstairs by Max Farnham

May 2001 – Clint Moffat, shot by Ron Dixon

March 2002 – Kitty Hilton, natural causes

20 BROOKSIDE FACTS

1. The first line ever spoken in *Brookside* was by actor John Whitehall who played a milkman doing his rounds. For the 1000th episode he was invited back to the programme to make another cameo appearance.

2. *Brookside* was the first 'soap' to repeat its episodes in an omnibus edition.

3. When shooting her final scene as Edna Cross in 1984, actress Betty Alberge found it very difficult to 'die' and instead kept opening her eyes during the take. In addition to playing Edna, Alberge has a unique place in the history of soap, appearing in the very first scene in the opening episode of *Coronation Street* in 1960.

4. During the early days on Brookside Close, shooting was regularly interrupted at 5pm by the chimes of an ice-cream van winding its way through the housing estate.

5. Simon O'Brien, who played Damon Grant, has admitted that when they were doing scenes around the dinner table in the Grant family's house, he and Paul Usher (Barry) used to compete to try and stuff as much food into their mouths as possible.

6. Close curmudgeon Harry Cross nearly turned out very differently. When *Brookside* was first conceived his character was to be called Alec and was described as 'an active 67 years… a very outgoing person [who] gets on well with most people.' Plus, the character was originally going to suffer a fatal heart attack after just a few months in the Close.

7. Assistant Floor Manager Francis Harcombe 'played' heroin addict Nicholas Black's body when it was carried away in a body bag.

8. Sheila Grier, who played Sandra Maghie, also ran a successful knitting business while she appeared in *Brookside*.

9. Jimmy Corkhill's character was originally only written in for six weeks, but Dean Sullivan proved such a success the programme kept him on permanently. Similarly, Michael Starke who played Sinbad originally made only a cameo appearance, but made such an impression that he was invited to take on a regular role.

10. One of the two men who followed Sheila Grant and Kathy Roach home in 1988 was played by Steve Halliwell, who would later appear as Zak Dingle in *Emmerdale*.

11. In 1988, the *Brookside* cast joined the cast of *Coronation Street* to make an appeal for donations during ITV's 'Telethon' campaign.

12. In 1990, the actors who played the Rogers family helped launch the British Dyslexia Society's Awareness Week at the House of Commons. At the same time on screen, *Brookside* was running a storyline dealing with Geoff Roger's learning difficulties.

13. *Brookside's* 1000th episode as billed in 1992 was not actually the 1000th episode produced for the series. Although *Brookside* episodes are numbered sequentially, when the programme had its first five-nighter over Christmas 1988, the additional three episodes were not included in this system. The following Christmas the programme enjoyed a third extra episode and this too was excluded from the count. This means the famous episode '1000' was actually episode 1004!

14. The Jury Room of *Brookside's* court set (built for the Jordache trial in 1995) doubled as the Thai customs office when Lindsey and Mike were arrested in Thailand for drug smuggling.

15. Jimmy Corkhill's dog Cracker was actually owned in real life by Tina Malone, who played Mo McGee.

16. Grant's restaurant was located in Mersey Television's staff canteen.

17. Appearing on *Desert Island Discs* in 1996, ex-*Brookside* writer Jimmy McGovern picked the theme to *Brookside* as one of the pieces of music he'd take with him to his fantasy paradise.

18. Mark Moraghan, who played Greg Shadwick, had previously appeared as one of the 'Scousers' (a thinly veiled parody of *Brookside's* Terry Sullivan) in Harry Enfield and Chums.

19. Jimmy Corkhill's website, as featured in the programme, was actually launched on the web in 2001 at www.jimmycorkhill.com.

20. *Brookside* has also been seen in Australia, Eire, Finland, France, Gibraltar, New Zealand and Switzerland, amongst other countries.

20 FAMOUS CAMEOS IN BROOKSIDE

1. Russell Grant (as himself, 1985)

2. Paula Yates (as herself, 1986)

3. Pope John Paul II (as himself, 1987)

4. Morrissey (appeared as himself in *South*, 1988)

5. Sarah Greene (as herself, 1992)

6. Lorraine Kelly (as herself, 1993)

7. Ken Campbell (as Oscar Dean, 1993)

8. Paul Barber (as Greg Salter, 1994)

9. Duggie Brown (as Ray Piper, 1994)

10. Loyd Grossman (as himself, 1994)

11. Lily Savage (as herself, 1994)

12. Brian Murphy (as George Manners, 1995)

13. Michael Parkinson (as himself, 1995)

14. Faith Brown (as Anne Bradley, 1996)

15. David Seaman (as himself, 1998)

16. Linda Lusardi (as Frankie, 1999)

17. The Nolans (2000)

18. Graham Norton (as himself, 2000)

19. Carol Smillie (as herself, 2000)

20. Les Dennis (as Jeff Evans, 2001)